FANTASTIC FOLKLORE AND FACT

Also by Edward Rowe Snow

Incredible Mysteries and Legends of the Sea

Tales of Sea and Shore

Astounding Tales of the Sea

The Fury of the Seas

Unsolved Mysteries of Sea and Shore

Mysterious Tales of the New England Coast

True Tales of Pirates and Their Gold

True Tales of Buried Treasure

FANTASTIC
FOLKLORE
AND FACT

. . . .

New England Tales of Land and Sea

EDWARD ROWE SNOW

ILLUSTRATED

DODD, MEAD & COMPANY   *New York*

Fourth Printing

Library of Congress Catalog Card Number: 68-54451
Printed in the United States of America
by The Cornwall Press, Inc., Cornwall, N. Y.

To DR. ROBERT E. MOODY
who, more than a quarter of a
century ago, taught me the importance
of accuracy and truth

INTRODUCTION

Centuries ago, when dictionaries as we know them today were coming into being, folklore, legends, and the like were handed down from generation to generation. The word *folk-lore,* however, was first suggested by W. J. Thoms, writing in the *Athenaeum* for 1846. Many students of language believe the word is an imitation of many German compounds such as *volksfest* and *volkslied,* but actually there is no real equivalent for folklore in the German language. The word did not become current in the English language until well into the latter part of the nineteenth century.

The Encyclopaedia Britannica in its Ninth Edition states that folklore is a "convenient though somewhat general heading under which to arrange all that has been observed or recorded of the traditions current among the 'common people' . . . whether in ancient, mediaeval, or modern times. . . . An exhaustive account of the folk-lores of the world would be equivalent to a complete history of the thoughts of mankind."

New England is one of the richest regions of the world in folklore and legend, as well as in bizarre but true tales. I have attempted to choose from hundreds of examples some that have interested me the most, and trust you enjoy my selection.

The following people aided me materially in the preparation of this volume: Mrs. Charles Baker, Jack Beasley, Nina Beasley, C. Francis Belcher, Dorothy Caroline Snow Bicknell, Jean Bright, Mary Brown, James L. Bruce, Louise Coggins, Arthur J. Cunningham, Thomas Curtis, Jeremiah Digges, Walter Spahr Ehrenfeld, Leo Flaherty, Judson Hale, Marie Hansen, Barbara Haywood, Melina Herron, Stillman Hobbs, Thomas Johnson, William Robert Kelson, Ben Kennedy, Joseph Kolb, Gary Kosiusko, Mrs. Marguerite Lechiaro, John McCarthy, William McIntire, Patricia McKenna, Muriel A. McKenzie, Joel O'Brien, Ruth Phinney, John Pyne, William Pyne, Laurence Rideout, Karen Rydwanski, Robb Sagendorph, Sgt. Paul Schwalbe, Bob Shaw, Tom Smith, Winthrop J. Snow, Joan Spunt, Carl W. Sternfelt, Nancy Stone, Russell Stone, Janet Sumner, Howard Tripp, Elgina T. Whitcomb, and Charles R. O. Wood. I owe a special debt of gratitude to Francis Xavier Joseph Moran.

My wife Anna-Myrle aided me on problems in almost every chapter, and her efforts in preparing the index were outstanding.

EDWARD ROWE SNOW

CONTENTS

ILLUSTRATIONS

Following page 84

PART ONE

. . . .

Strange Tales

CHAPTER 1

. . . .

MYSTERIES ON GEORGES BANK

A beautiful new Essex-built schooner, the *Charles Haskell*, became involved one March day almost a century ago in a combination of circumstances that ended in spectacular death at sea. The scene was the North Shoal, part of the dreaded Georges Bank, out to sea from New England's shores.

On the morning of March 6, 1869, the men on the schooner were hauling cod aboard in record numbers. From the deck of the *Charles Haskell* the sailors noticed that similar activities were taking place on every one of more than three-score craft in the vicinity. The fishing was so good that the crew members were actually having a desperate struggle to get all their catches aboard. One Gloucester fisherman in particular was terribly worried about what the wonderful fishing really meant.

"The last time this happened," explained Manuel Fernández, "a terrible wind hit that very night. That wind, mark me well, caused trouble."

Shortly before one o'clock the wind hauled to the easterly. Then, minute by minute it increased in intensity. By four that afternoon Captain Clifford Curtis, fearing what might be ahead, suspended the fishing, and ordered all men to haul in and prepare for trouble from the coming gale.

Letting out ninety fathoms of cable, the fishermen then took in the foresail. The captain ordered it reefed before furling in case the *Haskell* went adrift. The wind now began to whistle in that ominous, shrill tone which always indicates high velocity, and this caused the master to make a decision.

"All hands on deck," came his order. Three reefs were quickly taken in the mainsail, but by nine that night the gale had changed to a violent hurricane. Later it was estimated that more than three hundred vessels had been on Georges Bank at the start of the storm, many of them having the fearsome North Shoal dead ahead in the east-northeast wind then blowing.

Aware of the danger, Captain Curtis stood by the anchor cable, axe in hand. Although his anchor was still holding, he watched schooner after schooner slide by him on the way to possible disaster. The *Haskell* began to drag anchor, but suddenly she brought up short, the hook hitting an obstruction on the bottom. There she hung, giving and "tauting" by turns. Suddenly the forward lookout yelled a warning, for there, right over the bowsprit, a light was riding. Smashing his axe down on the cable, the master watched his craft slide around and the lights of the unknown fisherman pass harmlessly by, ten feet away.

The captain now decided to get to leeward of the others if he could, and work his way out beyond the North Shoal. Twenty minutes later he was carrying out his plan, but suddenly he saw a light on the weather bow. Incorrectly believing the other craft was anchored, the master of the *Haskell* ordered the helm put hard up.

Before he realized his mistake, the two schooners smashed together. The *Haskell* crashed down into the unknown vessel abaft the port rigging, splitting the stranger almost to the mainmast and breaking her own bowsprit. The two schooners then pulled apart, but the next giant wave lifted the *Haskell* high above the other fisherman, dropping her with tremendous impact on the other schooner.

Although in that moment of disaster several from the luckless fishing vessel could have leaped aboard the *Haskell* and saved their lives, none did. A moment later fishermen and schooner vanished forever.

Unbelievably, damage to the *Haskell* above the deck was confined to the broken bowsprit. The crew cut the mast off, tied a line to the jibstay, and passed the line through the hawsepipe, continuing it under the windlass.

Terribly afraid of what he would find, Manuel Fernández went below. He was almost certain that the craft was sinking, for no one aboard the *Haskell* expected she could possibly stay afloat after the terrible collision. In two centuries of Gloucester history no other vessel had ever lived through a collision in such a hurricane. Reaching the forecastle, Manuel found Elmer Woodberry, who was almost beside himself with joy!

"She hasn't a drop in her," cried Elmer. "Why, I don't know!"

Manuel ran up on deck to tell the master, but Captain Curtis did not believe him and ordered the pumps tested at once. The master soon ascertained that the *Charles Haskell* was not taking in a drop of water!

Now that the danger was over, the master began to think of the unknown fishermen on the other craft, whose graves would forever be the sea.

"I wonder if anyone caught her name!"

Unfortunately no one had. Later, when the storm ended and they reached Gloucester, they learned that nine fishing craft had been lost in the hurricane that night. Six of the nine were identified, and so it was agreed that the craft which the *Charles Haskell* rammed and sent to the bottom was either the *A. E. Price,* the *Martha Porter,* both of Gloucester, or the

Andrew Johnson of Salem. Captain Curtis knew the skippers of all three.

The *Charles Haskell* was run up on the flats near her owner's wharf, repaired, and refitted. While she was there, thousands came to look at her. Old fishermen could scarcely believe the story that she had survived a collision on Georges Bank. What she did, no other vessel had ever done in the history of Georges, and as far as can be told, it has never happened again.

W. H. Bishop decided to make an investigation and was able to discover by interviewing sailors of Salem that the craft struck by the *Haskell* was the *Andrew Johnson* of Salem.

After the *Haskell* was repaired and made ready for sea again, several of the older men in her crew decided that they had other plans. Shaking their heads, they told Captain Curtis that they were finding new berths.

Captain Curtis didn't laugh at the old men. On the contrary he turned upon them in angry fashion. "There is no blood on my hands," he shouted.

Nevertheless, two crewmen refused to ship with him, and the skipper had to find men for their places. All the others sailed with Captain Curtis, and on her next trip out, she ran straight down to Georges and came home with a staggering load of codfish.

Unfortunately, every man asked for one of the early watches, but then they always did that. The captain now conducted the time-honored custom of "thumbing the hat." The crew formed a circle, each sailor holding the brim of the hat, thumb up. The skipper closed his eyes and touched a thumb. Then Captain Curtis counted ten more thumbs, clockwise. The tenth thumb meant first watch. From then on counterclockwise, each man being given his choice until the entire crew was divided into watches throughout the night.

One night almost a week later, Manuel Fernández and

Oscar Richards took their midnight watch. At about quarter past twelve, Oscar tapped Manuel on the shoulder. He pointed forward, where Manuel saw a little group of men.

"Why don't they turn in?" Oscar asked.

"My God," cried Manuel. "They are not our boys!" As he watched, two more men joined the little group. The two men on watch noticed another man climbing in over the rail, and then another, and still another. Shadowy shapes in the form of men were climbing aboard the *Haskell* from out of the sea.

"Look!" Manuel whispered. "They come aft!"

As Manuel watched, it became apparent that the beings, whatever they were, paid no attention to the men on watch. The two men stayed at the wheelbox while the shadowy figures fished for nonexistent fish. Below deck the new watch was called, and Manuel and his watchmate went below and climbed into their bunks. Ten minutes later came the cry, "All hands on deck." When Manuel reached the deck, every crew member was staring at the shadowy forms going through the motions of hauling their lines.

The crew of the *Charles Haskell* now openly rebelled against staying on the grounds, and the skipper gave in at last.

"All right, boys, you win. Get in the anchor. We're going home."

Twenty-four hours later, homeward bound, during the same watch, the silent shadows again boarded the *Haskell*. She came abeam of the twin lights of Thacher's Island and just before dawn brought Eastern Point Light abeam and then bore about for Gloucester Harbor.

The schooner ran fast for Gloucester, and the skipper held her to her course. Then, and only then, did the figures mount the rail and step over the side.

Whatever the sailors saw, the fact remains that from the morning she arrived home from Georges Bank, the *Haskell* was taboo in Gloucester and Captain Curtis could not get a crew to take her out.

Manuel was the only one in the crew who would sail, but even he had a condition. "The next time we go to Georges," he told the skipper, "we don't take the vessel back to Gloucester but to Salem, where the crew we sent to the bottom lives. We take them home first!"

But the captain, a man of a colder, more practical race than Manuel Fernández, did not understand, and for months the *Charles Haskell* lay idle at a Gloucester wharf. Finally, rather than keep her at a dead loss, her owners sold her off to a group in Digby, Nova Scotia.

Whether the wanderers of Georges Bank ever came aboard the *Charles Haskell* again, I do not know. I have been told that in the year 1893 word reached Gloucester that the schooner *W. B. Keene* had picked up a box belonging to a hand-horn of the type used by fishing vessels for giving fog warning. On the box, which had been newly split and was but a few days in the water, was painted the name *Charles Haskell*. The *Keene* had been fishing for haddock on Georges Bank.

CHAPTER 2

. . . .

SALEM'S DOOMED SHIP

During the last half of the seventeenth century, the good people of New England became strangely excited by a belief that the powers of darkness had been let loose to work dire havoc in their ranks. Their religious leaders accepted many of the superstitions of the day, for witchcraft was solemnly recognized, and to doubt it was regarded as proof of religious infidelity and disobedience.

It is said that credulity is contagious, and so it is that the confused horrors of a few weak and fear-stricken minds were often shared by the entire population. The colonist who feared the face of no mortal foe, trembled like a child at the thought that when he walked in the forest his footsteps might be beset by evil beings not of this world. Bewildered by fear, their confusion building higher and higher, many New Englanders began to feel that the earth, air, and ocean teemed with the supernatural. The hoot of an owl was understood to be the mocking cry of a sprite, while often the roar of a midnight tempest became the howl of a legion of demons.

Men began to see armies battling in the air, and in the middle of the night would hear the sound of drums and trumpets. Sometimes they noticed the flights of fiery arrows streaming across the midnight sky. Although today we would call the arrows shafts of the Aurora Borealis, still they bothered the "souls of the gazers." The Reverend Cotton Mather often recorded such scenes in his *Magnalia Christi Americana.*

During this period, at a small inn at Salem kept by Hezekiah Peabody, a pious and righteous citizen, a seafaring man waited while the vessel of which he was the captain was being made ready for sea. From the window of his chamber, Captain Mark Walford could at any time have a view of his *Noah's Dove,* a large ship freighting for England. Though conforming in every particular to the Puritan style of dress, wearing a "sad colored" doublet and cloak without ornament, still he possessed a "marked individuality."

Shaggy, black eyebrows overhung his deep-set eyes, and hard lines were drawn across his ruddy cheeks. Two fanglike teeth projected from his lips. Visible even through his thick, grizzled mustache, they gave him the expression of a bulldog. Although no one could approach him without a shudder, there was no real fault to find with his behavior. He was a churchgoer, rigidly kept the Sabbath, and maintained the strictest discipline among his crew.

But sometimes, late at night, Deacon Hezekiah Peabody heard Captain Walford walking to and fro in his apartment with a heavy step, as if he was treading the deck of his ship. At such times the captain would give utterance to the deepest groans that ever came from a human breast.

Once when Deacon Peabody ventured to suggest to his strange guest that he could send for a clergyman to ease his mind, he was rebuffed by the ferocious expression in the captain's face. The innkeeper did not renew the subject, for it was really none of his business, and his guest always paid his reckoning punctually in good bright Spanish doubloons. However, Peabody told his wife in confidence that he feared the captain was troubled with an evil spirit. Mrs. Peabody soon told her neighbors about her husband's thoughts, and before long there was an uneasy feeling all over town about Captain Walford.

The *Noah's Dove* somewhat belied her name, for she mounted six guns and was provided not only with a formidable number of heavy Spanish muskets, but with a liberal supply of cutlasses as well. It was rumored that the excessive armament of the *Dove* was well out of proportion to the possible danger of meeting pirates on the ocean.

Several persons had engaged passage on board the ship. Strange to say, these individuals refused to listen to any of the mysterious murmurings around Salem against the captain. It appeared as if they were just as prejudiced in his favor as the others were against him.

Such was the state of things when Mr. and Mrs. Walter Severn, a young married couple, strangers in the town, arrived and took lodgings at Deacon Peabody's, after which the young man had engaged passage for himself and wife on board the *Noah's Dove*. The husband was handsome and engaging, while his lady was a ravishing beauty. She was not of Saxon origin. Her accent and, above all, her dark olive complexion, raven hair, and black eyes indicated she was from either Spain or South America.

The deacon's wife received her somewhat coldly, for the young Mrs. Severn, when cross-questioned about herself and her husband, took refuge in her ignorance of the English tongue; though at dinner time she could "find enough English" when she wanted any dainty dishes.

The men learned as little from Severn as the women did from his beautiful wife. Though affable and chatty enough on matters of general report, he wrapped himself in a sort of fierce reserve whenever the residents of Salem asked him about his own affairs. A singular incident connected with the couple was that from the moment of their arrival at the Peabody Inn, Captain Walford fled aboard his ship. Having seen their arrival from his chamber window, he sought out the landlord, threw him several doubloons, and immediately went on board.

Finally Friday, the day of sailing, arrived. All seafaring people in the town, thinking of the usual superstitions, remonstrated against Friday as unlucky, but the captain declared that he would sail that day "in spite of the Devil."

This profane statement completely ruined his reputation in the minds of the good people of Salem, who declared that the captain was given over and sold to the evil one. His was a "vessel of wrath," they claimed, and he was doomed to destruction, together with all his ill-fated crew and passengers.

But neither prayers nor entreaties or arguments could shake the confidence of those who engaged passage on the *Noah's Dove*, and amid the wild lamentations of their friends, they planned to sail with the captain. The vessel lay at anchor some distance from the wharf, and the embarkation was carried out by small boat.

The ancient oarsman who rowed the young couple to the ship declared that the skipper was a fiend, and that he had seen fire coming from the captain's eyes and nostrils. Having cast off his sober Puritan attire, the skipper now wore a doublet of carmine velvet and gold, with a satin cloak, a hat and feather, sword and pistols. His crew members were similarly attired, and indeed they looked more like buccaneers of the Spanish Main than peaceful, God-fearing mariners. When the boatman dared to suggest to the captain that he ought not to go to sea in such threatening weather, the captain told him to mind his own business. The master added with an oath that it was a fine topsail breeze, but as the boatman explained later, even a landsman could observe that the wind was fitful and about to freshen to a gale. The boatman added, moreover, that when the young Spanish bride reached the deck, she cast her eyes upon the captain and then instantly fainted. In that condition she was carried into the cabin by her husband.

The boatman's story circulated rapidly from mouth to mouth among the hundreds assembled on the pier, and increased the interest with which the townspeople watched the movements of the *Noah's Dove*. Then, just as the anchor was weighed, a black crow flew down and perched upon the maintop, uttering a weird croak. This incident excited the spectators, and from that moment the vessel was regarded as the "Doomed Ship." Soon she sailed out to sea and eventually over the horizon.

That night a storm arose, known forever afterward as the Gale of 1676. It was so terrible that the like of it was not remembered by the oldest settler in Salem. Chimneys were blown down, shutters torn from their hinges, and some of the largest trees sent crashing down because of the strength of the storm. For two days and nights the gale raged with unabated fury, and most of the residents of Salem decided that the *Noah's Dove* must have gone down in the hurricane.*

Four days later, as Cotton Mather wrote, a ship was seen coming up the bay. Everyone rushed to view the spectacle. A large ship she was, covered with canvas from deck to truck.

Though a strong gale was blowing directly off the shore, she came up in the very wind's eye, with all her sails full as if sailing with a fair breeze. Suddenly a stream of fire seemed to run down the mainmast, then a cloud of smoke arose, the sails disappeared, and, like some soft metal exposed to the heat of a furnace, yards, spars, rigging, and hull melted and sank, leaving in a moment the surface of the bay "clear and smiling" as before.

The horror-stricken spectators returned to their homes con-

* Salem had a similar sailing in 1802, when three craft, the *Ulysses*, *Brutus*, and *Volusia*, left the harbor together and were all lost on Cape Cod.

vinced that they had seen a symbolic representation of the fate of the doomed ship.

The *Noah's Dove* never reached England or any other port. Many, many years afterward—when almost her very name had been forgotten—an old gray-haired and sorrow-stricken man came to reside in Salem. He attempted to live the life of a hermit, but the day had gone by when a man could reside in Salem and retire completely from his fellow man. The piety and benevolence of the stranger made him respected, and soon several of the residents included him as their friend.

On his deathbed he is said to have revealed to a clergyman that his name was Walter Severn, and that he was the sole survivor of the *Noah's Dove*. His wife had been a Spanish lady, and she recognized the captain at the moment of sailing as a buccaneer by whom her father had been slain during an attack in the Gulf of Mexico.

Though he had resumed some of his old nefarious habits, the pirate-captain would undoubtedly have carried the ship safely to England if she had not met disaster. In the midst of a storm the *Noah's Dove* was struck by lightning and burned to the water's edge before sinking.

The overcrowded boats swamped and sank. Mr. Severn and his wife, floating on a spar to which they had lashed themselves, were saved by a Spanish bark bound for Hispaniola. Then, two months later they were able to sail to England. There, having the misfortune to watch his wife take ill and die, Walter Severn had sought to overcome his grief, and he returned to Salem to spend his declining years.

CHAPTER 3

. . . .

BOSTON LIGHT'S WEIRD WOMAN

I seriously doubt if I will ever understand all the implications present in this story of the weird woman of Boston Light. It was told to me by a sincere-minded follower of spiritualism, who explained that unless one believed in the supernatural, the story could offer vexing problems. I must admit that I have no solution as to what really occurred.

Little Brewster Island, where Boston Light stands today as the oldest beacon in all North America, has had many unusual activities in addition to the well-known lighthouse duties of the men at the station.

For example, according to James Lloyd Homer, in the early 1840s a "Spanish" cigar factory was located at the light, with young girls from Boston as workers. Another occupation that flourished at this time and continued for several generations was the boarding of summer visitors at the light. In addition, Joshua Snow, Boston Light keeper in the year 1844,* conducted such a successful boardinghouse that he soon gave up his lighthouse duties and moved across to Gallop's Island, where

* For details see my *Mysterious Tales of the New England Coast,* pp. 134–136.

15

his clam and fish chowder became known all over New England. Nevertheless, the origin of the famous Snow's chowder dinners was at Boston Light in the year 1844.

The story of the weird woman of Boston Light, however, is a far cry from Snow's chowders. Eighty-five years ago in the summer of 1883, when Keeper Joshua Bates was in charge, a young married couple, Mr. and Mrs. Philip Chardon, came out to the light. Although the official records do not mention the following story in any way, without question the tale should be included in this book.

At the lighthouse there were two bedrooms set apart for guests, and one of these was occupied by Mr. and Mrs. Chardon, who were boarding at Little Brewster Island. One day lighthouse keeper Bates told the couple that the empty room would be filled late the following evening, and that the future occupant would sail out from Hull. He was coming from New York by horseback and was originally from across the ocean.

The Chardons retired for the evening, but when they arose the next morning, the stranger was already at breakfast. As the lighthouse keeper was not much for formality, no introduction took place before or during the meal, but it was revealed that the visitor was Mr. Edward Moraine. Chardon estimated that Moraine was somewhere near fifty years of age, and realized that he was unusually handsome. Marie was fascinated by Moraine from the beginning, and her husband, who rarely saw her attracted by any other human being, was delighted to notice that she was listening intently to the breakfast table talk, although she did not speak herself.

After breakfast, as had been arranged, the lighthouse keeper took Chardon out fishing for lobsters. Chardon's wife and Mr. Moraine stood on the steps of the dwelling and watched the others as they rowed out from the calm water inside the double pier to the ocean. Moraine, although invited, had excused himself from the trip because, as he explained, he wished to rest from his long horseback ride of the day before.

Suddenly Marie turned to him. "Why did you come here?" she asked. It resembled the question of a little child and her voice had a strange, hesitating tone. "There is nothing for a man to do here," said Marie. "I sit on the wharf or go out on the ledge across from Shag Rocks. My husband finds that dull, and I suppose it is."

"Yes, perhaps that is so," said Moraine.

The two stood for a minute or two in silence. Then they separated.

Restless the entire morning, Marie took her shawl and the book which she never read to the private, cavelike nook under the cliffs which she had discovered the day of their arrival. Her mood was such a strange one that she soon put down her book and shawl. Noticing the low tide, she went down on the slippery boulders, which were heavily encrusted with rockweed, and a short time later she was at the very edge of the water. As Marie stood there she saw Moraine walking thirty feet above her on the nearby cliff.

"Would you like to join me?" she asked.

The two soon were sitting where she had left her shawl and book. In some way Marie began to feel that she had known this man for many years, although he had only arrived at the island twelve hours before. Her manner became so unusual that Moraine suddenly spoke up.

"Is it possible, Mrs. Chardon, that I have met you before? Indeed your voice sounds as familiar to me as my own. I am told that you have lived all your life in the United States, but that confuses me. I have a feeling we have met somewhere else."

"Indeed, I have the same feeling," she answered. "You tell me that you have been away from America for many, many years before you landed in New York. How can we possibly know each other? Of course, my life is a mystery. I feel as if I had been happy once. I shouldn't tell you this, but it is true. Indeed, I have no knowledge of my existence before meeting Philip!

"I like to be by the sea because, in spite of the fact I cannot remember, I seem to be closer to my past when I am on the shore. That is why Philip brought me here. I hate to be with anyone else while I am on the edge of the ocean."

"That means I should go, I suppose," answered Moraine.

Marie, however, put out her hand. "For some reason I can't understand, I want you to stay. Besides, I have a strange urge to visit that ledge out there. Could you possibly row me out? I know it's silly, but I have a wild idea that it may help me solve the confusion about my early life."

Ten minutes later Moraine was rowing Marie toward the dangerous Shag Rocks, the ledges which have caught many luckless vessels in their cruel tentacles.

Moraine brought the rowboat through the calm water until they were close to a canal-like crevice in the ledges. Then he rested his oars.

As they drifted along on the outgoing tide, the two paid more than passing attention to the various ledges and pinnacles. Marie had the strange feeling that she had been there before.

Meanwhile the sun described its parabola in the heavens and the shadows began to lengthen. Moraine rowed back to the lighthouse slip and the couple went across and down to the cavernlike niche.

A short time later Philip returned to the island with some fine lobsters, but when he brought them up to their room to show Marie, he could not find her. Knowing her favorite nook, he went down over the rocks, where he found her deeply engaged in conversation with Moraine, as though the latter were a very old and dear friend. The three returned together, but Philip did not speak until they reached their room.

"Marie," he said, "I am pleased that you find Moraine agreeable, but I think five hours with him is almost too much. It isn't what you should do with a perfect stranger."

"Philip, if you say so, I shall never do it again. Right now, I am terribly confused."

The remainder of the day passed without incident, but when the next morning came, they discovered that the warm, calm weather had done a turnabout. A driving rain was falling, which chilled the summer boarders. In addition to the downpour, a thick fog had set in, hiding from their view all the other islands of Boston Harbor. The seagulls began their plaintive cries, which mingled with the noise of surf battering the rocky ledges.

"This looks like the usual three-day northeast storm," said Mrs. Bates, the keeper's wife.

"Well," answered Philip, "to me it looks like a good day to spend indoors."

Standing up, he walked across to the window, where he could see the fog roll in. The rain continued to slide down the glass. Moraine put on his heavy boots and raincoat and walked out across the ledges beyond the lighthouse.

Inside, Philip watched Marie as she went to the window. Suddenly he noticed her start up, with her eyes showing animation. Edward Moraine was walking back toward the lighthouse, completely drenched by the storm. Philip now realized for the first time how strikingly handsome Moraine really was. Then he watched Marie as she began moving toward the door.

"Where are you going, Marie?"

"I don't know. Leave me alone." Marie quickly sank down on the divan, and lapsed into silence.

Rebuffed, Philip sat down near the shelf of books, took a volume, and began reading. Suppertime came, and the lobsters were enjoyed. After dinner they put several pieces of driftwood in the parlor fireplace and the wood was soon blazing and crackling. Outside the wind began to moan even more noticeably than before. The surf from the giant waves could be seen hitting above the top of the cliffs beyond the light. Every so often a giant billow would roll right up and through the low valley between the keeper's home and the lighthouse itself. Masses of spindrift flew out of the sea to lodge in deep foam all over the island.

Marie then announced that she was retiring for the night. The two men, left alone, sat close to the hearth and stared into the fire. Hour after hour passed, and the wind outside reached an even higher pitch.

"I am afraid that the lifesavers will have work tonight," observed Philip. "Have you ever seen such a storm?"

"Strangely enough, I have," answered Moraine. "I have been out as much as most men have in storms at sea, but have reason to remember a terrible gale some twenty-two years ago, right in this area."

"Tell me about it."

"I have never told this to anyone," began Moraine. "That night gave me a horror of the seas, and for twenty-two years I have tried to wipe away the terror. That is one reason I arranged for a visit to Boston Light, to view the scene of a terrible disaster which occurred at the rocks in the distance."

Suddenly the two men heard a shrill cry right outside the window. A seagull caught in the wind hit the pane and fell dead on the porch. A moment later another cry, this time of a human, came from inside the house.

"Edward, Edward!" Marie then stepped into the firelight and stood before them. Both men jumped to their feet. Neither spoke a word, for even as they watched, Marie's face appeared transformed. It seemed like that of another woman. It was not Marie any more, for apparently a stranger had taken the place of the woman who was Philip's wife. Moraine's voice then broke the silence.

"My heavens," he whispered.

Marie stretched out her hands to touch Edward, who then collapsed into his chair. The woman went down on her knees beside him.

"My dear, now I know who you are!"

A full minute passed without a sound from inside the room.

"Edward, have you forgotten? I was your wife Alice, so long ago. Twenty-two years. I am sure you remember that night, that terribly black night, full of shrieking voices and the groaning and grinding of the wreck on those awful rocks, and the waves which crashed down on us, tearing us apart. Thus you see, Philip, why I can never love you, yet indeed I was your wife."

"Marie!" shouted Philip Chardon, and turned to the other man. "What have you done to us?"

Ignoring Chardon, Moraine now spoke. "Do you remember how we parted?"

"Yes, I do," said the girl. "It all is clear now. When a wave came rolling over, you said, 'For one minute, Alice. It doesn't take long to die.' "

Edward stood up. Philip caught Marie's hand, but she twisted away. Then with a sharp cry, she fell as though dead. The two men picked her up and a moment later Philip slowly carried her to their room.

Several hours later, just before dawn, Edward Moraine still sat in the parlor by himself. The fire was ashes and the lamp was almost burned out. The house had been very still since Philip had taken the senseless woman up to their bedroom.

Suddenly there was a footstep and Philip rushed into the room. "Moraine! Good heavens, she is not here either. My wife has vanished!"

The two men dashed out of the room. Both instinctively

knew where to look for her. Reaching the ledge over the cavernlike area in the rocks, they suddenly saw her. She had gone out in the storm and had reached a ledge near the light. As they stared at her, they noticed that her long, loose robe was twisted about her body. Then a mighty wave began to form in back of her. It came roaring in, hitting the ledge with a tremendous shock, and when it went down, they saw the rock and the sea, but Marie had vanished.

They waited for her, but began to realize she would never come back.

"I have lost her forever," groaned Philip. "I never understood her and now I shall never know why!"

"Indeed you are right," said Moraine, with his eyes fastened on the troubled seas. Morning began to dawn on the ledges at Boston Light.

CHAPTER 4

. . . .

THE LADY OF GREENBUSH

There are several islands along the coast between Boston and Plymouth, each of which has its own history during the time of occupancy since the days of the Pilgrims.

H. Leavitt Horton, author of *The History of Hingham,* first told me the story of the Strange Lady of Greenbush. He said that in 1911 when he was a very young lad, his mother was hospitalized and passed away. He mourned her passing for some time and finally decided to leave home forever. Packing his bag, young Horton headed for Greenbush. His uppermost thought was to visit the old summer home at Trouant's Island, where he and his parents had spent the month of July in 1908.

About one in the morning, clad in a sheepskin coat and carrying the heavy suitcase, young Horton stepped off the train at Greenbush to begin a long walk down the tracks. As he walked over the bridge, he began to feel a great sense of loneliness as the train whistle and the click of wheels faded into the distance. Reaching Damon's Point, he walked over to the road leading to Trouant's Island, and an hour later found the building there. Erected on the edge of the marsh, the small summer cottage was cold and damp, but young

Horton went to bed between clammy sheets and was soon asleep.

Suddenly he was aroused by the sense of a presence. He could hear a deep sobbing and moaning, accompanied by a swishing sound. It drew nearer and nearer, but finally the swishing stopped. A tall, thin woman entered the room, paused, then slumped into a chair near the table.

In the pale light of the moon her face had a classical beauty but was so thin as to be almost skeletal. She was wearing a long dress with sleeves which were tight at the wrists, and a high lace collar. The top part of the dress was a sort of vest which buttoned tightly at the waist. The skirt fell in drapes around her like a shroud, and it was this skirt which had made the swishing sound as she walked through the long marsh grass.

"This is my wedding dress," she said. "It is very heavy and I can't stand it much longer. My boy," she added, "you have been weary, but now your mind will be at peace." Pointing to the river, she said, "Go to the little spring down by the river and get some water."

He looked for the spring and found it just as she had said. In the distance he noticed a sailing craft. It was an old black sloop drifting toward the open sea. There was no sail and no sign of anyone aboard.

When he returned to the shack, he found the Lady gone, and so he packed his bag and started for the train, again observing the old sloop out beyond Third Cliff, Scituate. When he last turned to look back, the sloop had entirely disappeared.

Later Mr. Horton told his father the story of his trip to Greenbush. His father said he had walled up the spring when they stayed at the hunting shack in 1908, and the dress as described by Mr. Horton was exactly like the one his mother had worn when traveling, although he had never seen it.

Because of the publicity given the island ghost and also because of the fact that no one now living can be affected in any way, I now tell for the first time of an incident which may be closely connected with the lady ghost of Trouant's Island.

The only promise I made to the storyteller is that I would not publicize unduly the principal characters in the tale. If anyone has a desire for more particulars, I'll supply him personally without publicity.

About the year 1916 a man and his wife decided to live on the island. One night, when the man was unable to return to the island because of an unusually high tide, the woman heard a very strange noise in the lower part of the residence.

For those who have not been over to Trouant's Island, it is located at the mouth of the North River close to Scituate's Fourth Cliff and across the river from Third Cliff. When the tide is high it is almost impossible to reach the island without a boat, unless you wish to swim. Actually at the time of the incident there were four feet of water over the causeway which leads out from Marshfield to the island. The lady's husband could not possibly risk slipping off the causeway in the darkness to fall into watery depths of ten and twelve feet, which exist at high tide on each side of the corduroy road.

His wife locked herself in their bedroom until three o'clock in the morning, at which time the man returned. By then the tide had gone down enough for him to hike out over the causeway in ankle-deep water. Reaching home, he was amazed to find that his wife's lamp was still glowing in the parlor.

She greeted him with enthusiasm, and told him of the strange noises. They went down below, where they had never entered before, and found a pile of canvas sails which without question had recently been disarranged. The husband pulled at the sails, revealing to his horror the skeleton of what obviously had been a woman. For the remainder of the early morning darkness they debated about what to do. Finally he resolved to dig a grave in the soft earth outside the house and bury the skeleton then and there! Three hours later his task had been completed.

The family left the island without telling any one what had happened. Both have passed on since the incident and there is no way at this late date of even guessing why the wife heard the noises, or who the skeleton had been in life, and why it was in the half-basement of the summer cottage.

CHAPTER 5

· · · · · · · · · ·

GHOSTS ABOARD THE

LUCY JACKSON

Scores of weird, mysterious tales have been narrated at sea in the graveyard watches of the night by veteran Gloucester fishermen to the younger members of the crew. I am not referring to the outright yarns which on occasion are told to impress and scare the listeners, but rather to the stories in which the fishermen implicitly believe. The tale of the *Lucy Jackson* is in the latter category.

As Charles Skinner told the story over a century ago, the *Lucy Jackson* was such a splendid craft that it was hard for the Gloucester people to understand why she changed owners so often. Somebody would buy her, fit her for a run to the Banks, then suddenly sell her for less than she had cost him. When the *Lucy* had been sold four times in about as many weeks, the men of Gloucester demanded that the reason be made known.

The *Lucy*, it was learned, had a ghost. The various owners, of course, were quiet about this because the word "ghost" is apt to injure the value of property. They tried to sell before damaging rumors had gone abroad too far.

Everyone in Gloucester knew of the ghost by the time the

Lucy had been sold for the third time, and when the seventh transfer came within three years, it is said that almost every fisherman on Cape Ann was aware of the *Lucy Jackson's* visitors from another world.

Indeed there was no question but that several people had seen a white figure that moved about the deck and entered the cabin to lose itself among the smells and shadows of the hold. This was said to be no dream, no invention of nervous persons, for it had been seen by fishermen not usually affected by sea superstitions.

The last purchaser was Jake Davenport. "What do I care for ghosts?" he asked. "I have sailed with them often enough, and would rather have them aboard any vessel of mine than rats. They say the *Lucy* lost some of her men on the Banks—drowned, you know. Well, if it's any comfort to the poor devils to keep their berths with us I guess we can let them stay so long as they keep middling quiet and don't hurt our luck."

Brave words. They may have been no more than throat deep, for old Jake Davenport knew, as well as anybody, that he would have a hard time shipping a crew aboard any craft that had ghosts in her hold. He went down to the wharf to see his prize and attempted to estimate what it would take to put her into the best condition. He "botched around" till night fell and the harbor front was deserted. A melancholy fog came in, dulling the few lamps to be seen ashore, and so he lighted a lantern and continued his explorations. She was a lonesome tub, he had to admit. He also decided the mice, rats, and roaches emphasized the loneliness more than usual. He found the forecastle, smelling of stale pipe smoke and moldy boots, in a dreadful state and he began to pile up old boxes, pannikins, and torn oilskins, intending to pitch them overboard.

Suddenly he was interrupted by a groan. Standing motionless, Jake listened intently, and then he began to relax, for what he heard was merely the schooner rubbing against the timbers of the wharf. Possibly the wind was coming up. He would just gather the rubbish and come around in the morning to finish clearing up, because his lantern might go out if he stayed aboard.

At that moment he heard the groan again! Jake felt a sudden chill, and for a moment his legs refused to move. He kept control of himself, however, for giving way to panic wouldn't help. The groan came again, this time from below deck. Climbing down the narrow, greasy companion hatchway, Jake held the lantern above his head and looked around. It was deserted. There was a faint roll in the water, with the noise of choppy gurgles from under the wharf—nothing else. Going aft, he found that he had left his pea jacket in the cabin. Putting it on, he started to go home. Hardly had he passed the hatch when an awful groan was heard, and something in white came slowly up the ladder.

Captain Jake's scalp started to slide back. His eyes began to pop, while his mouth pulled open in a grin of abject terror. In a frenzy he clutched a swordfish lance that was lying on the deckhouse. Recovering his speech, Jake began to swear in exceptionally vigorous sea language.

The specter was on the deck, groaning and reaching toward him. Taking careful aim, Jake flung the spear at the dread visitant. Throwing up its hands, the ghost fell to the deck with a shriek. This seemed human and substantial, and therefore comforting. Jake ventured nearer and put his lantern close to the mystery. It wore boots—number tens. It was also bleeding, for the spear had grazed and cut its neck. It was also swearing. Captain Jake gave a tug at the white wrappings, and they came off, considerably bloodstained. Then he stood erect and began to speak.

"Abe Dimmock, you durned old fool! What are you doing in them duds? This is pretty business for a grown man to be in, ain't it? And you the skipper of this very boat, once. I'm surprised, I am, and I'm good and ashamed on ye. Say, you do look most sick enough for a ghost. Guess I must have scratched you, eh? Well, I've got my flask of Medford rum. Take a pull, and I'll tie up your neck. You can say a prayer while I'm a-doing it, if you've a mind to, along of not being killed outright."

A little later the former captain of the *Lucy,* bandaged and comforted, was taken home. There he confessed that he had been playing ghost to bring a bad name to the schooner, so that her cost be brought down to three thousand dollars, the amount he had saved. Eventually he recovered, sailed aboard the *Lucy Jackson* as mate, and was drowned off the Cape some years later. Since becoming a real ghost Abraham Dimmock has not been seen on board at all.

CHAPTER 6

· · · · · · · · · ·

THE PHANTOM BOAT

In keeping with the general tone of this section of the book, I offer the following poem, written by E. Norman Gunnison several generations ago.

THE PHANTOM BOAT
A Legend of Cape Ann

The tide comes in and the tide goes out,
  And the rollers break on the harbor bar,
And up from the distance comes a sail,
  Gleaming white 'neath the morning star.

Fishing tackle and boats on deck,
  Running rigging belayed and trim;
Raking spars—'tis no battered wreck
  Sailing out in the distance dim.

It draws not near, though the wind is fair;
  The sheets are free, but it comes not nigh,
But hangs, a point on the morning air,
  A pictured sail 'twixt the earth and sky.

Fisherman, tell me why yonder boat
  Sails, and no nearer comes to shore;
Nor in the distance grows remote—
  Not a ripple her bow breaks o'er.

"Stranger, I reckon you aren't here long,
  Many a year has her pennant flew—
Old is the story—a worn out song—
  But her deck is trod by no mortal crew.

Look a moment and see the flame
  Gleaming white over mast and spar—
Here! take my glass, you can read the name
  Under her starn—'tis the 'Alice Marr.'

Alice Marr was a fair young girl,
  Long ago, in Glos'ter town;
Rippling ringlets and sunny curl,
  Rare red lips and a cheek of brown.

That was Alice, the fisher's pride;
  Lovers sought her, from near and far;
She was John Ackman's promised bride—
  He named his vessel the 'Alice Marr.'

Thar's nothing sartin, stranger, in life;
  We're gone to-morrow, though here to-day,
Another v'age she would be his wife—
  At least, so I've heard the gossips say.

Pork, potatoes and hard-tack stowed,
  Water in barrels and water in tanks,
Nicely fixed for a three months' cruise,
  He sailed away for the fishing banks.

'For men must work and women must weep,'
  Men must work for their daily bread;
One month out—all well on board,
  Spoke by the 'Dart' of Marblehead.

Months rolled on, and never a word;
  Six months, twelve months—on the day
That finished the year was a rumor heard
  Of the 'Alice Marr' in the outer bay.

Boats put out, but they drew not near;
  Slowly, silently on she steered;
'Skipper Ackman! ho! what cheer?'
  She had vanished and disappeared.

Ever as rolls the year around,
  Bringing again her sailing day,
Rises her hull from the depths profound,
  And slowly cruises the outer bay.

Not a word of her master's fate,
  Only a glimmer of sail and spar;
Not a word of her crew or mate—
  This is the ghost of the 'Alice Marr.'

Still *she* watched down the peaceful bay,
  Still *her* eyes scanned each gathering cloud,
Years receded, and worn and gray,
  Her wedding dress was her fun'r'l shroud."

This is no myth of the poet's pen,
  This is no mirage upon the blast,
The boat *is* there, just the same as when
  Mine own eyes saw in the Summer past.

Only the eye of faith *can* see,—
  Eyes are blinded—and this in brief—
What is holden from you or me,
  Is seen by others who have belief.

Still in the morning, cold and gray,
  Gazing afar the sea to scan,
Looking out from the sheltered bay,
  See the phantom which haunts Cape Ann.

PART TWO

. . . .

Facts

CHAPTER 1

. . . .

LIZZIE BORDEN, NEWBURYPORT
AND TIMOTHY DEXTER

Newburyport is indeed a fascinating area to visit. I have
spent hours and hours in the cemeteries of this city looking
for and finding the gravestones of outstanding personalities
who have interested me. Indeed I have come to feel guilty if at
least once a year I do not visit the grave of shipbuilder Donald
McKay at Oak Hill Cemetery. This world-famous clipper-ship
expert is buried in the family lot there high on the sloping
hillside.

A short distance away in the same cemetery is the gravestone of author Edmund Pearson, who died in 1937. Pearson
wrote many books on true murders, his masterpiece being his
volume *Lizzie Borden.**

A few years ago detective-story writer Edward D. Radin
decided to challenge Pearson's book about Lizzie Borden,
and visited my office to examine a confession which I have,
believed to have been signed by Lizzie Borden. Later he wrote
his own volume † in which he proved, at least to his own

*Lizzie Borden, on August 4, 1892, is believed to have murdered her step-
mother, Abby D. Borden, and her father Andrew J. Borden, with a hatchet.
Tried, she was acquitted.

 † Edward D. Radin, *Lizzie Borden, the Untold Story,* Simon and Schuster,
1961

satisfaction, that Lizzie did not kill her mother and father. Radin claimed that the actual criminal was Bridget, the servant of the household.

On my last visit to Newburyport, in 1968, I thought of the poetry written about Lizzie, the most famous of which found its way into both Pearson's and Radin's books, and into my chapter on the subject in *Piracy, Mutiny and Murder*. Later I shall quote this world-famous quatrain about Lizzie Borden, which was probably written in 1893. Since then many other verses concerning the tragedy have appeared.

In 1967 Dick Smyser, Managing Editor of the *Oak Ridger*, Oak Ridge, Tennessee, produced some doggerel on Lizzie. The first was a quatrain as it "might be written under today's prevailing journalistic practices."

> The Bordens, Emily and Max
> Were found dead Tuesday, slain by axe.
> Police say eighty blows were sledged,
> Their daughter did it, it's alleged.

The second, according to Dick Smyser, was as it might be under proposed new pretrial publicity guidelines.

> A terrible thing has come to pass
> At the Borden home in Fall River, Mass.
> Involved are father, mother, chile;
> For further details attend the trial.

Here is a Quincy, Massachusetts, version:

> Lizzie Borden and her sister Emma
> Knew the truth of this tragic dilemma.
> Writers three—Pearson, Snow, and Radin—
> Never could pin it to this Fall River maiden.

The famous 1893 quatrain, which has been translated into many tongues, follows:

> Lizzie Borden took an axe,
> And gave her mother forty whacks,
> And when she found what she had done
> She gave her father forty-one.

One of the finest books on the entire Lizzie Borden controversy, *A Private Disgrace,* was written by Victoria Lincoln in 1967. This volume should set at rest the minds of millions of people who, up to the time of the printing of the book, were in doubt as to Lizzie's guilt. No fair-minded individual can read the book and still claim that Lizzie was innocent.

Another cemetery in Newburyport, the Old Hill Burial Ground, contains a "distinguished" tombstone in the graveyard. It is the stone of "Lord" Timothy Dexter. As Samuel Adams Drake wrote in 1883, "Timothy Dexter was not born great, neither did he have greatness thrust upon him." Nevertheless, even today, after the lapse of well over a century and a half, many visitors to Newburyport ask first of all to be guided to the Kelson-Jackson-Dexter House where the renowned Lord Timothy lived.

Timothy Dexter was not a native of Newburyport. The honor of being his birthplace is claimed by Malden, Massachusetts, where a branch of the family occupied one estate for more than a quarter millennium. Although bred to the tanner's trade, Timothy was far too shrewd to remain a "lowly tanner." Dexter became ambitious, believing that a key of gold would permit him to unlock the door which led to the circles of aristocracy. Newburyport was a center of culture, refinement, and literature, and Dexter was eager to attract attention to himself by living in a beautiful Newburyport mansion. Finding two estates available for his purpose, he couldn't make up his mind and bought both of them. Almost from the first he was dissatisfied with the State Street mansion, and soon moved out. Nevertheless, he sold it at a substantial profit.

Dexter then moved to the estate on High Street, which was more to his liking. Before he finished remodeling, it was one of the truly different mansions of Essex County. He did attract the attention of the socially prominent residents of Newburyport, but not favorably. Vain to excess, he practically begged for the adulation which some people are always ready to lavish upon those who are more wealthy than they are.

When he realized that he wasn't "arriving" socially, he decided to carry out a plan which would make his name known and remembered long after that of the most important socialite of the generation had been forgotten. Strangely enough, he was successful, for his plan has never been carried out anywhere in the world before or since that time!

His renovation eventually transformed the estate which his predecessor had built into a conglomerate patchwork of confusion. Working under his directions, the painters gave the outside of the edifice a coat of brilliant white and trimmed it with green. Next the carpenters moved in and built minarets upon the roof in the center of which rose a lofty cupola surmounted by a golden eagle.* Standing as it did upon the crown of the hill, the house dominated the scenery for miles around, and soon became a landmark for mariners far at sea.

Lord Timothy now carried out his most fantastic innova-

---

* William Robert Kelson, the present owner of the Lord Timothy Dexter house, had the golden eagle taken down in 1956 or 1957, as it needed restoration. He told me that for personal reasons he will never put it back on the roof of the cupola. The famed eagle, four feet high with a width of thirty inches, has a position "at the alert" with wings drawn back. It is made of four pieces of pine, a solid piece for the body, two separate pieces for the wings, and a special piece for the tail.

tion, an exhibition which would forever engrave his name in the pages of Newburyport history. Visiting a young, talented Newburyport ship carver named Joseph Wilson, Lord Timothy told the artist that he wanted his mansion surrounded by statues of famous people. Not only did he want the statues about eight feet high, but he desired them placed on unusually tall pedestals as well.

Gladly did the sculptor accept and execute this order, for it enabled him to lay the foundation of a small fortune and to acquire a lasting reputation among his townsmen for his superior workmanship.

Most of the statues were conscientious reproductions of real people. The carved clothing was painted to resemble that worn by the actual personages—blue coats, white shirts, buff breeches, and the rest—altogether making a display which no museum in the entire country could equal.

The statue of Quincy's great president, John Adams, was in a prominent position over the main entrance to the house. There Adams stood bareheaded in the presence of George Washington, who stood in the center. Dexter explained that no one should be covered on the right hand of his greatest hero, General Washington. On the left of Washington was Thomas Jefferson (his hat on), holding in his hand a scroll inscribed "Constitution." Lord Timothy, in spite of the painter's objections, insisted upon spelling the name of the Sage of Monticello "tomas," instead of "Thomas." He finally threatened to shoot the artist on the spot if he persisted in his refusal.

The man who had planned and created this garden of statues had a mind which often changed overnight. If he raised a statue to some favorite with whom he became displeased, he reserved the right to change his name as soon as the fancy struck him. Frequently a stroke of the painter's brush transformed statesmen into soldiers or soldiers into civilians.

If a statue represented General Daniel Morgan on one day, it might well be Napoleon Bonaparte the next. Incidentally, Dexter always paid his respects to Napoleon by touching his hat in salute whenever passing the great Corsican's statue.

On the panel of each column was inscribed the name of the person represented by the statue. Among the individuals depicted were Governor John Langdon of New Hampshire, Governor Caleb Strong of Massachusetts, Rufus King, General Butler of South Carolina, General Knox, John Jay, John Hancock, William Pitt, Louis XVI, King George, Lord Nelson, and the Indian chief Corn Planter.

One allegorical figure depicted maternity while another represented a typical traveling preacher. Two enormous lions occupied pedestals along with the men.

Dexter himself was twice represented. One of his statues stood near the door holding in its hand an inscribed placard reading, "I am first in the East, the first in the West, and the greatest philosopher in the known world." The cost of these representations with the columns on which they were placed is said to have been fifteen thousand dollars, the equivalent of one hundred thousand dollars today.

This was the only way, however, in which Lord Timothy was able to bring himself into association with greatness. Society never accepted him, for it is possible that his vulgarity was too much even "for all his gold to gild."

Having a house and grounds which he flattered himself would make his not-so-fortunate neighbors green with envy, Dexter next resolved to set up an equipage fit for a lord. One which suited his ideas of magnificence was accordingly procured. Someone had told him that the carriages of the nobility were always decorated with a coat of arms. He immediately ordered one composed and painted on the panel.

In the matter of horses Dexter was fastidious and capricious, as author Samuel Adams Drake tells us. As soon as the Lord grew tired of one color, he would sell the animals at extravagantly low prices and purchase horses of another color. His costly carriage, drawn by beautiful animals, became one of the sights of the day. The spare figure of Dexter, sitting bolt upright, his hairless dog squatted beside him, offered such a contrast that whenever the carriage passed through the town it provoked quite a little laughter. Boys of the day would mockingly shout for everyone to "clear the way for my lord's carriage!"

In this coach Dexter once was forced to drive to the County Prison at Ipswich where he was given a fine for firing his pistol. He had discharged his gun in the general direction of a countryman who had stared at his museum of celebrities. The countryman had not moved when Lord Timothy commanded him.

Dexter did not consider his establishment complete until he appointed a poet to write Dexter's praises and to extol his virtues in verse. One Jonathan Plummer, an eccentric peddler of fish, was chosen. Having a gift for rhyming which many people who should know better called genius, Plummer was installed in Dexter's household as poet laureate.

A handsome new livery was ordered for the Newburyport poet. It consisted of a fine black broadcloth coat, with stars on the collar and a fringe on the skirt, shoes with large silver buckles, a cocked hat and a gold-headed cane. One of Plummer's poems to his patron has been preserved in its entirety. Excerpts follow:

> Lord Dexter is a man of fame,
> Most celebrated is his name,
> More precious far than gold that's pure:
> Lord Dexter shine forevermore!

> His house is white and trimmed with green;
> For many miles it may be seen;
> It shines as bright as any star;
> The fame of it has spread afar.
>
> Lord Dexter, like King Solomon,
> Hath gold and silver by the ton;
> And bells to churches he hath given,
> To worship the great King of Heaven.

Dexter now jumped from poetry to prose, his own prose in fact. Aiming at literary fame, he wrote and published his *Pickle For The Knowing Ones*. This autobiography has puzzled almost everyone who has read it. Unbelievably, the *Pickle* had immediate success. The spelling is atrocious, and there was no attempt at punctuation. The author corrected this defect in a second edition by inserting a page or more of punctuation marks at the end, with the following note:

> mister printer the Nowing ones complane of my book the fust edition had no stops I put in a Nuf here and they may peper and solt it as they plese.

Although most people believe this is the only case of its kind, the English humorist Tom Hood speaks of a similar instance, in which a friend of his offers punctuation as follows:

> And these are my points that I place at the foot,
> That you may put stops that I can't stop to put.

Dexter's unusual financial speculation of which he tells in his *Pickle For The Knowing Ones* was sending warming pans to the West Indies. For many years this story was accepted as truth. Nevertheless, William C. Todd in 1886 could not find any customhouse records concerning this transaction and thus believed that Dexter never sent any warming pans out of Newburyport. John P. Marquand stated in 1960 that all records were destroyed in a customhouse fire. Notwithstanding, the story of the warming pans has done more to make Dexter's name remembered than almost anything else. In addition to Todd, many other people considered the warming-pan yarn pure fabrication, designed for those inquisitive people who are continually asking how Dexter made his money.

But even if the story is too good to be true, as a merchant Dexter's shrewdness was proverbial and New England accepted it as the "lucky blunder of fortune's favorite fool."

In his *Pickle* book, Dexter tells how, having dreamed three nights running that warming pans would do well in the West Indies, he collected "no more than forty two thousand," which were put on board nine vessels bound to different ports, and cleared himself seventy-nine per cent. The story goes that one of Dexter's captains, being a shrewd fellow, took off the covers of the pans, which were then sold to the sugar planters, all of whom were anxious to obtain them for ladles.

Dexter's speculation in Bibles could also be doubted. Quoting his words, he dreamed that "the Good Book was run down in this country so low as half price, and dull at that. I had," he says, "the ready cash by wholesale. I bought twenty one thousand. I put them into twenty one vessels for the West Indies, and sent as a text that all of them must have one Bible in each family, or they would go to Hell."

Besides putting faith in dreams, Dexter believed in fortune-telling as well as fortunemaking, and on many occasions attempted to pry into the obscurity of the future by consulting the oracle of his neighborhood. She was one Madam Hooper, a strange character, who, after teaching school, assumed the profession of fortunetelling. The noted Lynn clairvoyant

Moll Pitcher also had Dexter for a patron, and her influence is said to have been beneficial.

One of the oddest of Dexter's freaks was his mock funeral, which was arranged with all solemnity years before his death. Wishing to create a sensation, Dexter built a spacious tomb in his garden. Then he had delivered to his mansion a costly coffin made of mahogany, richly adorned, for he wished to see the effect his funeral would produce on the townspeople. Invitations were issued, mourning apparel was prepared for his family, and someone was found to officiate as minister. After the procession was duly formed, the people marched to the vault in the garden. While this farce was taking place, Dexter was looking on from an upper window, and before the company had dispersed, he was found beating his wife for not shedding enough tears at his death.

Many people had actually attended the funeral thinking that Newburyport's most unusual character had died, and until they saw his effigy in the coffin, did not realize that here again was one of Dexter's tongue-in-cheek activities.

Of his personal life it is said that he became tired and dissatisfied with his wife. After offering his distraught mate two thousand dollars to leave him, he advertised for another wife. When no one applied, he decided that the wife with whom he had become displeased wasn't so bad after all, and gave her two thousand dollars to return to him.

On the twenty-sixth of October, 1806, Lord Dexter really died. The funeral from his High Street mansion was an occasion which would have pleased him to witness, but for sanitary reasons the town officers would not allow his remains to be deposited in his garden tomb. Therefore he was laid away among his fellow humans in the Old Burial Ground near the frog pond.

During the great September Gale of 1815, mentioned by Oliver Wendell Holmes as the one which blew away "my

Sunday breeches," the storm toppled the statues, and the Dexter House soon became dilapidated. About the year 1846, when it was being used as a factory boardinghouse, the estate was purchased by E. G. Kelley of Newburyport, who possessed both wealth and taste. Kelley proceeded to obliterate as far as possible all traces of his predecessor's eccentricities. The three presidents over the door were taken down and demolished, the grounds were newly laid out, and now very little remains to show Dexter's bizarre achievements in ornamentation or to moralize upon Lord Timothy Dexter's fantastic life.

William Robert Kelson, who now lives in the house, visited the Smithsonian Institution in Washington to see the only known existing statue from the mansion. It is supposed to be that of William Pitt, but the Institution has withheld complete identification because of a missing bill of sale. However, Mr. Kelson tells me that at the Newburyport Historical Society there is a wooden arm and hand of one of the statues which once adorned the estate of this unusual man.

Timothy Dexter was a unique personality who achieved what he most desired—attention. Today, 162 years after his death, few people in the area are unaware of his story, which cannot be said of those who attempted to ignore him. Perhaps that is the way Dexter wished it, after all.

CHAPTER 2

• • • • • • • • • •

AN ESCAPE FROM STATE PRISON

In 1934, while doing research for my book *Castle Island,* I first learned of the famous Massachusetts State Prison established on Castle Island in 1785, and of its subsequent removal to Charlestown, Massachusetts. I discovered the career of the escape artist, Stephen Burroughs, whom poet Robert Frost calls a preacher of "unsanctified sermons." Burroughs made many successful escapes, at least on one occasion taking the guise of a minister, at which time he used a pocketful of his father's sermons. His most spectacular flight from prison occurred at Castle Island.

Massachusetts had to wait for more than a century for the next escape artist from State Prison who could compare with Burroughs' efforts of 1785. The name of the man was John C. Leonard.

Leonard, or Lenny as he was called, had left home at twenty-three to join a gang of roving young Bostonians. Caught in a holdup, Lenny was sentenced to State Prison at Charlestown for five years in the year 1890. Once in jail, Leonard found that the prison was forbidding. This old-fashioned structure of solid stone had narrow, poorly lighted cells, primitive sanitary accommodations, solid steel doors, a paved exercise yard, and a twenty-foot wall surrounding the cell blocks and shops.

As has almost every other human similarly confined, Leonard looked around for a method of escape, but one veteran told him to forget it.

"Lenny," he advised, "it is out of the question."

Young and optimistic, however, Leonard paid no attention to the others and continued looking. Nevertheless, he was under no illusions and knew that it was one thing to yearn for freedom and another to win it. November had been the month of his incarceration, and soon the fierce New England winter enfolded the prison and the little world around it. In spite of this, Leonard decided he would be free when pleasant weather returned.

With the coming of spring Leonard and several others were assigned to work on the new wing then under construction. Lenny often looked up at the high walls, with the sentry boxes and the armed sentinels, and yearned for escape. In the back of Lenny's cell was the usual high barred window. He thought that if he could cut through the steel rods, he could escape. He then arranged with friends outside for his freedom.

Finally came the day when a saw was smuggled in to him. Within a few days he had cut through the steel rods and was ready to accomplish his escape. Four other men were to duplicate his performance a few minutes later, but when the break came, he escaped and they were caught. Leonard, soon over the wall by means of a grapple and a length of rope, found a change of clothes where his confederates had placed it near the prison, and was ready for the outside world again. Wearing his new suit, he reached the home of a friend. Later he arrived in Montreal and then took a cattle boat to Hamburg.

When the ship reached the German port, he received thirty-six dollars in pay for his work on the cattle boat, but he became sick in a Hamburg hotel. By the time he was well he had spent all his money. The only job offered to him came three months later when he signed aboard the *Normania* for a trip to New York with a cargo of toys. In October the ship landed in New York. When Lenny went ashore, and a policeman looked at him almost too intently, the guilty man signed on at once as a crewman with the next craft available, a sailing schooner bound for Liverpool. Running into a hurricane, she was forced to limp into Boston for repairs. As there was a reward of one hundred dollars for Lenny's apprehension, one of his shipmates who knew his secret turned him in, and before nightfall he was back in the Charlestown State Prison.

For the next half year Leonard was deeply involved in plans for carrying out another prison break. Of course, when the warden learned how John C. Leonard arranged his first escape, he assigned the convict to another part of the prison, the solitary ward, where he was not allowed to communicate with anyone at all. Then, as Leonard showed signs of penitence, the warden released him from solitary confinement and allowed him to return to a job in the yard. Leonard was a skillful mechanic and soon was back working with his mates on necessary repairs and reconstruction. A short time later he was talking with the others about another possible escape.

His fellow prisoners regarded him with special consideration for, in spite of what others would say, they knew that he had escaped from the State Prison and thus was on a special pedestal. One day a trustee told him that one of the oldest prisoners at the institution, a man who was under life sentence, was anxious to meet him. The lifer was so meek and mild that no one dreamed that he might even think of escaping. Nevertheless, the lifer carried around with him, between the layers of leather in the sole of his shoe, a fragment of parchment on which was a sketch of a way out of Charlestown State Prison.

Twelve years before, the lifer had served as a clerk in the

construction department where the plans for the new wing had been drawn up.

As was customary, the secret portions of the plan were in the warden's office. But the lifer was present when a general cleanup was in order. Many old records and accounts had to be gone over and then destroyed. Files and portfolios which went back for several generations were examined and the old lifer was given the task of checking them.

In his searching, the venerable prisoner discovered plans on parchment which had been used more than a century before in the building of the old prison. One sheet in particular stirred his imagination, and although he didn't understand it, he knew it was important. He hid the parchment in his shirt, and afterward placed it in an old volume on a dusty shelf in the office. When his health later failed, he was dismissed from the job, and the lifer transferred the parchment to his mattress. A short time afterward he fashioned a slit in his shoe for the plans.

The old man admired Lenny because the latter had escaped from State Prison. One afternoon, when rain drove them both indoors in the shed, the lifer confided to Lenny that he had the parchment plan. When Lenny showed interest, the lifer took off his left shoe, pulled up the lining, and removed the parchment.

"Watch the door," Lenny ordered, "while I examine the map."

Lenny put the map on the floor. Kneeling down, he oriented the parchment with the facings of the buildings and walls which he knew so well. Then he slowly deciphered its lettering and the meaning of the lines and curves. Suddenly a gleam of triumph brightened his features, for John C. Leonard now saw a way to escape again from the Massachusetts State Prison.

Leonard realized that the lifer could not capitalize on his

find, for the old man did not have the training to interpret the plans. Lenny was a mechanic, a mason, and a stonecutter, and was able to understand the lines and symbols completely. The key to escape on the parchment was the underground route of the sewer or drain, 215 feet long and 16 inches square. Buried twelve feet under the level of the prison yard, the sewer drain emptied into the river. If the men could find the sewer and break into it, they might be able to crawl through. Barring obstructions in the tunnel, they could reach the river and liberty.

Digging down to the drain unobserved, of course, was the greatest problem. Leonard was then transferred to the paint shop, which he estimated had been erected directly over the sewer. Unfortunately there were six others in the shop who had to be told of the scheme, and circumstances demanded the inclusion of two additional prisoners in the plot to escape. One of these, the eighth man to be made part of the scheme, was the messenger who was always running in and out of the paint shop with official messages.

The first step involved taking up the wooden floor in such a way that it could be put down again at a moment's notice. As they dug, the prisoners had to dispose of the piles of earth which came out of the pit they were digging. At first they put the dirt in with the regular rubbish, but when the rather stout individual who ran the prison dump detected much more earth in the sweepings than usual, he accused the men of plotting to escape. The prisoners were forced to reveal their plans to him, and his price for agreeing to stay silent was permission to join the escapers as the ninth man.

Work progressed faster now, for there were no restrictions on the amount of earth taken to the prison dump. Nevertheless, already four and a half months had been required to sink the hole the desired twelve feet.

Unfortunately, when the great moment arrived and the pit

The boat trip to Shag Rocks, off Boston Light. *(Pt. I, Ch. 3)*

Lord Timothy Dexter's mansion in Newburyport. *(Pt. II, Ch. 1)*

Opposite top: Charlestown State Prison, showing area used for the mass escape headed by John C. Leonard. *(Pt. II, Ch. 2)*

Opposite bottom: The Willey House. *(Pt. II, Ch. 3)*

Right: Abel Crawford, White Mountain sage. *(Pt. II, Ch. 3)*

Below: The Summit House on Mount Washington, which Dr. Ball never reached. *(Pt. II, Ch. 4)*

Sarah Bishop, the hermitess, outside her Connecticut cave.
(Pt. II, Ch. 7)

Opposite: The Old State House, Boston, showing window under balcony opening into offices of duelist Selfridge. *(Pt. II, Ch. 8)*

Black's aerial view of Boston, 1860. *(Pt. II, Ch. 8).*

Gull Head, off the Maine coast. Dead Man's Ledge may be seen from here at half-tide. *(Pt. IV, Ch. 1)*

The giant hermit of Isle au Haut with Henry Haggman in the fore-
ground. *(Pt. IV, Ch. 3)*

Henry Haggman at his moment of crisis with the treasure. *(Pt. IV, Ch. 3)*

Cape Elizabeth Light. *(Pt. IV, Ch. 4)*

Rescue of a survivor from wreck of the *Oakey Alexander. (Pt. IV, Ch. 4)*

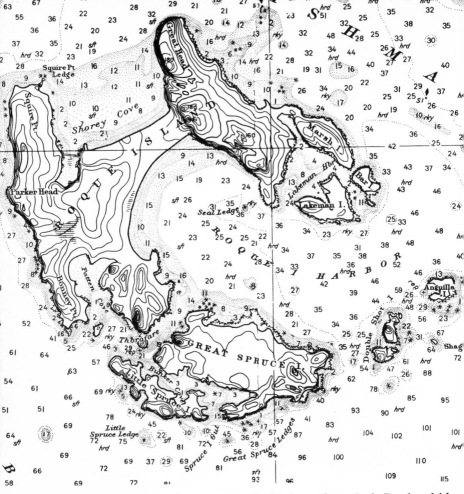

Roque Island area, off Roque Bluffs, Maine, where Jack Bunker hid the food vessel. *(Pt. IV, Ch. 6)*

Opposite: Boon Island Light, located ten miles out to sea from Cape Neddick Nubble in Maine. Photo by Howard White. *(Pt. IV, Ch. 8)*

Dorothy Snow on subchaser wreck between Humarock Beach and Marsh-field. *(Pt. IV, Ch. 9)*

Donald Hourihan showing grindstone from schooner wreck of 1830. *(Pt. IV, Ch. 9)*

The steamer *Portland* lost off Cape Cod on November 27, 1898, as painted by John H. Dodge of Kenyon, Rhode Island. *(Pt. IV, Ch. 10)*

CHAPTER 6

. . . .

THE RESCUE OF MOLLY FINNEY

One afternoon in 1949 when I was hiking down the coast from New Brunswick, Nova Scotia, I reached Freeport, Maine, where I first heard the story of Tom Mains and his sister-in-law Molly.

Mains settled in Freeport more than two centuries ago. By 1756 he had cleared several acres in Freeport and put up a comfortable cabin. Unfortunately he was not to enjoy his possessions for long. One night Indians came to the cabin. They killed him and one of his children, wounded his wife, and carried into captivity his sister-in-law, the pretty, lively Molly Finney. In the fighting, one of the Indians had been wounded by a shot. On the six weeks' march to Quebec, where the Indians usually collected the bounty offered for Yankee scalps and where they expected to sell their captive, the girl was compelled to serve as nurse to the wounded man. It is thought that she put more salt and tobacco than salve into the dressings for the wound, as the patient would often spring from his bed of pain with the most terrible howls and threaten to beat her. The other braves would always interfere, for they had to admire her pluck and pride. Nevertheless, they warned her that if the injured one died on the journey, they would surely kill her at the same time.

On reaching Quebec, she was sold to a man named Lemoine who treated her fairly but kept a close watch over her so that she would not escape. Her moments of freedom consisted of the time she spent sweeping dust from the walks. Molly was a good cook and manager, and when she went out from the kitchen into the enclosed back yard, she was noticed by Monsieur Beauvais, a softhearted neighbor who began to find reasons for frequent calls on the Lemoines. It was evident that Beauvais had discovered that Molly was extremely desirable.

Lemoine did not like this, and decided that in spite of his wife's jealousy, he would guard Molly from Beauvais. Lemoine continued to lock Molly in her room every night. One morning, however, Molly answered a knock at the front door and was confronted by a handsome Yankee, Captain Richard McLellan, whose ship had recently come into port for trading. She learned that hostilities were over now with the French and Indians, and both sides were more than eager to trade and make money. Before she could ask his errand, he surreptitiously handed her a note, motioning her to hide it at once. Later in her room she read the note, which told her that friends in Maine had commissioned the captain to smuggle her away from Quebec as quickly and secretly as possible. Through diplomatic inquiry Captain McLellan had learned where she was and how closely the people were guarding her. The note went on to say that he would await her reply at seven o'clock the next morning.

At the chosen time she was industriously sweeping the walk, and one of the things that was swept almost into the hands of Captain McLellan as he strolled by was a folded piece of paper which he casually picked up. He didn't read it until he rounded the corner, as he saw that Lemoine was glaring at the two of them from the doorway. The letter revealed the plan of the house, showed the position of Molly's room, and suggested eleven o'clock that night as the time for the escape.

Captain McLellan was under Molly's window at the appointed hour. He tossed up to her a rope which she made fast to her bed. Ten minutes later she was coming down the rope and soon was in his arms. They made their way through the deserted streets, and in a quarter of an hour the two were aboard the *Hepzibah Strong,* which by daybreak was off for her home port, Falmouth, Maine.

At just about the same time, Lemoine unlocked Molly's door. He knocked and called but there was no response. Opening the door, he found the room empty and a note pinned to her pillow. "Woman's will is the Lord's will. Good-day, M. Lemoine." Then he noticed the rope, and wondered if it could have been an elopement. Of course, he decided, that sneaking scamp Beauvais with his soft voice and smooth ways! Lemoine seized his cane and went immediately around to see his neighbor, and before the latter could offer a protest or explanation, he had given Beauvais a dreadful beating.

By this time far at sea, with Molly secure in his cabin, Captain McLellan was sailing the *Hepzibah Strong* in the general direction of Anticosti Island, which by dawn two days later he left astern.

A week went by at sea, and then Seguin Island came abeam. The wharves of Falmouth, Maine, came into view the same afternoon, and soon the *Hepzibah Strong* was tied up at her pier. Three months later Molly and the captain who saved her life were married.

CHAPTER 7

· · · · · · · · · ·

A NEW ENGLAND HERMITESS

For strangeness, the story of Sarah Bishop's life is probably unequaled in New England history.

Born in Cold Spring Harbor, Long Island, New York, some years before the Revolution, she was the victim of one of the British raiding parties during the year 1778. Seized and taken aboard a small British privateer, she became a member of the crew under degrading circumstances. As the weeks went by, however, she and the young captain of the privateering craft fell in love. From that moment on he defended her from the unwelcome attentions of the rest of the crew.

The captain, wounded in a later raid, was nursed back to health by Sarah. By this time Miss Bishop had become an active member of the crew and could handle the wheel with the expert touch of a real sailor. One day, however, during a battle between her ship and an American privateer she was separated from the captain and later learned that he had met his death in the engagement. She then made plans to get ashore from the craft at the earliest opportunity.

The chance did not present itself for six months. During that time she lost all desire to live, so wretched were the circumstances to which she was reduced. Then came a day in 1780 when the privateer was anchored off the shores of Stamford, Connecticut. Watching her chance, she came out on deck when the others were asleep, dropped over the side, and swam to the beach.

Reaching the shore in her wet clothing, Sarah made her way by the early daylight along the banks of the Mill River. She finally reached Ridgefield, Connecticut, where later she was seen by Samuel G. Goodrich, a famous writer * of the period. He was amazed by a visit to a cave she had discovered on a nearby hillside, and wrote as follows of her career.

"Men hermits have been frequently heard of, but a woman hermit is a rare occurrence. Nevertheless, Ridgefield, Connecticut, could boast of one of these among its curiosities. Sarah Bishop was, at the period of my boyhood, a thin, ghostly old woman, bent and wrinkled, but still possessing a good deal of activity. She lived in a cave, formed by nature, in a mass of projecting rocks that overhung a deep valley or gorge in West Mountain. This was about four miles from our house, and was, I believe, actually within the limits of North Salem; but being on the eastern slope of the mountain, it was most easily accessible from Ridgefield, and hence its tenant was called an inhabitant of our town.

"This strange woman was no mere amateur recluse. The rock—bare and desolate—was actually her home, except that occasionally she strayed to the neighboring villages, seldom being absent more than one or two days at a time. She never begged, but received such articles as were given to her. She was of a highly religious turn of mind, and at long intervals came to our church, and partook of the sacrament. She sometimes visited our family—the only one thus favored in the town—and occasionally remained overnight. She never would eat with us at the table, nor engage in general conversation. Upon her early history she was invariably silent; indeed, she

* 1793–1860.

spoke of her affairs with great reluctance. She neither seemed to have sympathy for others, nor to ask it in return. If there was any exception, it was only in respect to the religious exercises of the family: she listened intently to the reading of the Bible, and joined with apparent devotion in the morning and evening prayer.

"I have very often seen this eccentric personage stealing into the church, or moving along the street, or wending her way through lane and footpath up to her mountain home. She always appeared desirous of escaping notice, and though her step was active, she had a gliding, noiseless movement, which seemed to ally her to the spirit-world. In my rambles among the mountains, I have seen her passing through the forest, or sitting silent as a statue upon the prostrate trunk of a tree, or perchance upon a stone or mound, scarcely to be distinguished from the inanimate objects—wood, earth, and rock—around her. She had a sense of propriety as to personal appearance, for when she visited the town, she was decently, though poorly clad; when alone in the wilderness she seemed little more than a squalid mass of rags. My excursions frequently brought me within the wild precincts of her solitary den. Several times I have paid a visit to the spot, and in two instances found her at home. A place more desolate—in its general outline—more absolutely given up to the wildness of nature, it is impossible to conceive. Her cave was a hollow in the rock, about six feet square. Except for a few rags and an old basin, it was without furniture—her bed being the floor of the cave, and her pillow a projecting point of the rock. It was entered by a natural door about three feet wide and four feet high, and was closed in severe weather only by pieces of bark. At a distance of a few feet was a cleft, where she kept a supply of roots and nuts, which she gathered, and the food that was given her. She was reputed to have a secret depository, where she kept a quantity of antique dresses, several of them of rich silks, and apparently suited to fashionable life; though I think this was an exaggeration. At a little distance down the ledge, there was a fine spring of water, in the vicinity of which she was often found in fair weather.

"There was no attempt, either in or around the spot, to bestow upon it an air of convenience or comfort. A small space of cleared ground was occupied by a few thriftless peach trees, and in summer a patch of starveling beans, cucumbers, and potatoes. Up two or three of the adjacent forest trees there clambered luxuriant grape vines, highly productive in their season. With the exception of these feeble marks of cultivation, all was left ghastly and savage as nature made it. The trees, standing upon the tops of the cliff, and exposed to the shock of the tempest, were bent, and stooping toward the valley—their limbs contorted, and their roots clinging, as with an agonizing grasp, into the rifts of the rocks upon which they stood. Many of them were hoary with age, and hollow with decay; others were stripped of their leaves by the blasts, and others still, grooved and splintered by the lightning. The valley below, enriched with the decay of centuries, and fed with moisture from the surrounding hills, was a wild paradise of towering oaks, and other giants of the vegetable kingdom, with a rank undergrowth of tangled shrubs. In the distance, to the east, the gathered streams spread out into a beautiful expanse of water called Long Pond.

"A place at once so secluded and so wild was, of course, the chosen haunt of birds, beasts, and reptiles. The eagle built her nest and reared her young in the clefts of the rocks; foxes found shelter in the caverns, and serpents reveled alike in the dry hollows of the cliffs, and the dank recesses of the valley. The hermitess had made companionship with these brute tenants of the wood. The birds had become so familiar with her that they seemed to heed her almost as little as if she had been a stone. The fox fearlessly pursued his hunt and his gambols in her presence. The rattlesnake hushed his monitory signal as he approached her. Such things, at least, were entertained by the popular belief. It was said, indeed, that she had domesticated a particular rattlesnake, and that he paid her daily visits. She was accustomed—so said the legend—to bring him milk from the villages, which he devoured with great relish.

"During the winter she was confined for several months to her cell. At that period she lived upon roots and nuts, which she had laid in for the season. She had no fire, and, deserted even by her brute companions, she was absolutely alone, save that she seemed to hold communion with the invisible world. She appeared to have no sense of solitude, no weariness at the slow lapse of days and months: night had no darkness, the tempest no terror, winter no desolation, for her. When spring returned, she came down from her mountain, a mere shadow —each year her form more bent, her limbs more thin and wasted, her hair more blanched, her eyes more colorless. At last life seemed ebbing away like the faint light of a lamp, sinking into the socket. The final winter came—it passed, and she was not seen in the villages around. Some of the inhabitants went to the mountain, and found her standing erect, her feet sunk in the frozen marsh of the valley. In this situation, being unable, as it appeared, to extricate herself—alone, yet not alone—she had yielded her breath to Him who gave it. . . .

"Desolate in fortune, blighted at heart, she fled from human society, and for a long time concealed her sorrows in the cavern which she had accidentally found. Her grief—softened by time, perhaps alleviated by a veil of insanity—was at length so far mitigated, that, although she did not seek human society, she could endure it. The shame of her maidenhood—if not forgotten, was obliterated by her rags, her age, and her grisly visage—in which every gentle trace of her sex had disappeared. She continued to occupy her cave till the year 1810 or 1811, when she departed, in the manner I have described, and we may hope, for a brighter and happier existence."

Thus ends the story of the hermitess as told by writer Samuel G. Goodrich more than a century ago. Since then Sarah Bishop's story has been published by other writers at various times. Much has been written in regard to this hermitess, for as such she was known, and her life fully warranted and justified the appellation. The narratives and traditions in regard to the life of Sarah Bishop are generally uniform, and in a measure the cause of her death, the season in which it occurred, and the place generally agree. However, old residents in Ridgefield, still living, tell different tales related to them in their youth by the neighbors of the hermitess as to the details of her death.

George Lounsbury Rockwell, writing in 1927 in his *History of Ridgefield* states that although Mr. Goodrich spoke of her visits to the house of his parents as the "only place in town thus favored," he probably referred to the homes in Ridgefield village. The hermitess often visited neighbors on West Mountain and in South Salem. She also attended the Presbyterian church in South Salem. It is asserted that she kept a few fine dresses, some of them rich silk, at the home of Jared Hoyt, who lived on the corner of South Salem and Lake Waccabuc roads. The hermitess would stop here and exchange her old clothes for one of the fine dresses. Upon her return from church she would again stop, and discard her good clothes, and once more don her tattered garments.

"Sarah Bishop was loath to relate her early history," states author Rockwell. "It is known that she was of a good family, and that her home was on Long Island. It is believed that she selected her lonely home on West Mountain from the fact that a fine view of Long Island Sound could be obtained from the high point of land just above the cave. On clear days a wide sweep of the water stretched out before the eye and the Island itself was plainly visible. It is thought that the portion of Long Island thus seen was near the home of her girlhood days."

In the year 1810, or 1811, the sad life of the hermitess ended. History and tradition are at variance as to the time and cause of her death. The generally accepted story is that one stormy night she left the house of one of the neighbors, who lived on the corner of the road leading up to the mountain. Wending her way up the steep mountainside to her cave she fell and, too weak to continue her way, perished from the cold. She was found a short distance from her cave. Joseph Knapp, who lived near the state line, has related to his grandson Eben Bouton that he was one of those who discovered her lifeless body. She was found among the rocks beneath one of the grape vines which had overspread a large chestnut tree, a short distance down the hill from her cave. The hermitess was buried in the Episcopal Cemetery in North Salem. No stone marks her grave.

The poem of Samuel G. Goodrich shall end our thoughts on this strange woman.

> For many a year the mountain hag
> Was a theme of village wonder,
> For she made her home on the dizzy crag,
> Where the eagle bore its plunder.

> Up the beetling cliff she was seen at night
> Like a ghost to glide away:
> But she came again with the morning light,
> From the forest wild and gray.

> Her face was wrinkled, and passionless seem'd
> As her bosom—all blasted and dead—

And her colorless eye like an icicle gleam'd,
Yet no sorrow or sympathy shed.

. . .

Her house was a cave in a giddy rock,
That o'erhung a lonesome vale;
And 'twas deeply scarr'd by the lightning's shock,
And swept by the vengeful gale.

. .

And often she mutter'd a foreign name,
With curses too fearful to tell,
And a tale of horror—of madness and shame—
She told to the walls of her cell!

CHAPTER 8

• • • • • • • • • •

THE AUSTIN DUELS

One of the prominent families of New England, the Austins, are of interest to me in many fields of activity. On two occasions in the past, members of the Austin family were involved in dueling, both in the same year. One duel took place on March 31, 1806, and the other August 6, 1806. Then there was General Nathaniel Austin, a member of the Charlestown branch of the family, who attempted to cut a canal through a lonely island in Boston Harbor for small craft to use as a refuge in stormy weather. His father had purchased Outer Brewster Island in 1799, and the general hired stonecutters to make the canal, which was abandoned before completion. Another branch of the family moved to Maine, where two sisters spent the remainder of their lives taking care of more than two dozen cats in a never-finished castle in the woods.

Nathaniel Austin, Brigadier General of the Massachusetts militia from 1815 to 1820, was also high sheriff of Middlesex County at the time of the capture of highwayman Captain Lightfoot, the so-called "last of the highwaymen." It was Austin's task to execute Lightfoot by hanging him at Lechmere Point, December 20, 1821, for the robbery in October 1821 of Major John Bray on the Medford Turnpike.

My own connection with the Austin family began during the summer of 1932 when Mrs. Snow and I paddled our canoe down Boston Harbor to reach Outer Brewster Island. There we entered the so-called Austin Artificial Canal and explored the region where the stonecutters had worked more than a century before. We were later told that buildings were erected in Charlestown from material quarried at Outer Brewster.

Shortly after this I met Mrs. Walter Austin for the first time. She told me about the unusual family circle into which she had married. Later she gave me all the details which her husband had collected of the duels, and also the story of Peter Rugg, written by duelist William Austin, Walter's grandfather. Elsewhere in this volume I tell the strange story of Peter Rugg.

The duel between William Austin and James Henderson Elliot was fought March 31, 1806, less than two years after the memorable Hamilton-Burr duel of July 11, 1804. It is hard to realize that the period between the beginning of the century and the ending of the War of 1812 was one of extreme political beliefs, passions, and prejudices. Party feeling ran high, and the many duels fought during these years often originated from some obscure political quarrel.

As was the case in the Hamilton-Burr conflict, the origin of the Austin-Elliot duel was political. Both were young men. Democrat William Austin was twenty-eight, and James Henderson Elliot, a Federalist, had barely attained his majority. Elliot was the challenger, acting on behalf of his father, Major General Simon Elliot, who had allegedly been wronged by Austin in a newspaper article which Austin signed "Decius."

Born March 2, 1778, William Austin was the son of Nathaniel Austin of Charlestown, where the Austins had settled in 1638. Graduating from Harvard College in 1798, he took up law as a profession.

In 1799 William was a chaplain in the Navy and is said to be the first commissioned chaplain in the service. Four years later he studied law at Lincoln's Inn, London, returning in eighteen months to practice his profession in Charlestown.

Austin acquired an early interest in politics, was elected to represent Charlestown in the lower branch of the State legislature and the County of Middlesex in the Senate.

Classmate Sidney Willard tells us that Austin's ideas indeed "were quick and often brilliant, but his temperament was impulsive, and he failed in that degree of illustrative amplification and that continuity of thought which are necessary to lead common minds to the desired conclusion."

Austin became one of eight members of the 1798 class at Harvard who were members of the State Convention of 1822.

Austin was elected a member of the Phi Beta Kappa Society but "did not accept, declaring his determination not to belong to any secret society."

When he became a judge and officiated in trials for the County of Middlesex, "all the Boston Bay, with scarcely an exception, brought their Middlesex actions to his Court."

Though a lawyer, Austin appears to have been as deeply interested in his avocations as in his vocation, and foremost among these was the writing of books.

His story of Peter Rugg, printed in the *Galaxy* (a paper published by Joseph T. Buckingham) had great sale and was copied in many newspapers and miscellaneous journals. It is a story unsurpassed in its field.

The story of "Peter Rugg" especially gained Austin much popularity, and the editor of Buckingham's *New England Galaxy* says of it: "This article was reprinted in other papers and books, and read more than any newspaper communication that has fallen within my knowledge."

The high character of Austin's work was recognized by one of the foremost of American critics, a scholar well acquainted with the history of American literature, Colonel Thomas Wentworth Higginson. In an essay contributed to the *Independent*, March 29, 1888, Colonel Higginson speaks of William Austin as "a precursor of Hawthorne."

Captain Joseph Loring, an officer in the State militia, was arrested because he disobeyed a brigade order given him by General Simon Elliot, a Federalist. The trial of Loring, a Democrat, began October 29, 1805, and was in reality a political matter, with the newspapers taking sides according to their affiliations. Thus we see that in this period politics entered even into the army. On December 7, Captain Loring, who had been imprisoned all this time, was acquitted of the charge. Unfortunately he was kept in jail and not even informed of his acquittal, and a letter of complaint to Governor Caleb Strong did nothing to help him.

Meanwhile the pages of the Boston newspapers were not lacking in comment. On March 17, 1806, there appeared in the Democratic *Independent Chronicle*, a letter from "Decius," * addressed to General Elliot. The message was a long one, and excerpts follow:

> Do you know, Sir, that every moment you have thus contemptuously holden Capt. Loring under arrest is *false imprisonment* for which you yourself ought to be arrested? A soldier's honor ought to be dearer to him than his life. . . . I speak in behalf of every freeman in the state; *for the degradation of the*

* Decius was a Roman emperor from A.D. 249 to 251. He was in favor of censorship and against Christians.

soldier in a free country is the first step to tyranny. . . . Sir, you are not a man destined to do any good or much harm, otherwise than as your setters on may push you beyond their own responsibility.

DECIUS

Decius also indicated in the letter that his real name could be obtained by a visit to the newspaper. General Elliot read the letter, visited the newspaper and obtained Austin's name, after which, on March 20, 1806, he allowed the Federalist *Boston Gazette* to speak of the "infamous attack" in the *Chronicle* on General Elliot. Elliot met Austin on Court Street, Boston, and began to assault Austin, but the latter more than took care of himself, and Elliot was badly beaten in the encounter.

On March 18 Henry Sargent * told Austin that "young Elliot" expected satisfaction, unless Austin would apologize. Austin immediately refused.

Elliot's son, James, hearing of his father's unfortunate encounter, now took over the affair and arrangements were made for a duel between Austin and James Henderson Elliot, to be fought at sunrise, March 31, out of the state, to avoid penalties then present in Massachusetts.

On March 30 principals and seconds left Boston by stage for Providence, where they all spent the night. Meeting the next morning at Cold Spring, now a part of Providence,† the two men fought with pistols at ten paces. The seconds were Mr. Sargent for Mr. Elliot, and Mr. Charles Sumner, father of Senator Sumner, for Mr. Austin.

The depth of feeling on both sides is indicated by the fact

---

* Henry Sargent was the artist of the painting now in the Hall at Plymouth, the *Landing of the Pilgrims,* known to millions.

† Cold Spring was between Pitman and Waterman streets, close to Pitman, and between East River Street and Bellevue Street. The spring was filled in about 1899.

that no less than three shots were fired by each duelist, instead of the two the articles of agreement called for. Austin was wounded in each of the first two exchanges, and as blood had been shed, honor was satisfied even after the initial exchange. Struck first in the neck when his own pistol misfired, Austin at the next exchange was hit in the thigh. Both men missed on the third encounter, after which the parties immediately left for Boston. Actually, Austin's wounds were superficial, while Elliot had not been hit.

The subsequent history of the two men might be claimed a paradox. Austin, wounded twice, lived to be sixty-five, dying on June 27, 1851, while the victor, who survived unharmed, lived barely two years after the encounter, dying in April 1808.

The second duel of the same year in which members of the Austin family participated came about because of an incident on the Fourth of July. The Republican Party of Boston had arranged a procession for July 4, 1806, with a banquet to be held afterward in a tent at Copp's Hill in the North End of Boston. All went well during the parade, but when it became known that the ambassador from Tunis would be attending the banquet in the tent, scores of people without tickets stormed the tent, and in the confusion the ticket taker was overwhelmed. Upward of one hundred persons without tickets "crashed the gate." Two particular items for which the caterer had not been paid I shall never forget. They were, according to the Jefferson Tavern landlord who had supplied the feast, "seven roast pigs and ten bushels of green peas." When the payments were in, he found that he was far short of making expenses and put the bill in the hands of Boston attorney Thomas Oliver Selfridge.

The attempts of Selfridge to collect the shortage by suit against the committee as individuals ultimately failed.

When the head of the committee, Benjamin Austin, was being questioned one day about the suit he answered that it was instigated by the Federalist lawyer Selfridge. The latter, who had an office in the Old State House, at the head of State Street, stated that Austin was mistaken. When it was proved to Austin that Selfridge had not been responsible for the suit action but had merely served as the lawyer in the matter, Austin retracted, but not with the sufficient enthusiasm needed to pacify Selfridge.

Thomas Selfridge now wrote a letter to the *Boston Gazette* in which he called Austin a "coward, a liar, and a scoundrel." Austin followed with a counter statement, and matters reached a crisis.

The details of this unusual duel are buried in the realm of obscurity. On August 6, 1806, in the middle of the day, Thomas Selfridge put his affairs in order. He then took a pistol from a drawer in his desk, left his room in what is now the Old State House, and started walking down the middle of State Street. He reached a point no less than ten feet from the location where the 1770 Boston Massacre had occurred. There he had expected to confront Benjamin Austin, but it was Austin's son who was awaiting him.

Eighteen years of age, Charles Austin was a student at Harvard College. Having chosen to act for his father, Charles had armed himself with a rattan cane.

The two slowly approached each other. Then, before Austin was actually able to strike his opponent, Selfridge cocked his gun and fired, mortally wounding the Harvard youth. The lad managed to get in a few feeble blows with the cane before he collapsed, after which he was carried inside Mr. Townsend's shop nearby. Descendants of those who lived in Boston at the time still argue as to whether Selfridge, a relatively feeble man, shot Austin before Austin had a chance to strike him with the rattan cane. In any case, after being treated by Dr. Thomas Danforth, Austin died.

Selfridge was accused of the murder, as there had been many who had watched the encounter. The trial began before Judge Isaac Parker on November 25, 1806. Testimony of two important witnesses of the encounter follows, the first being that of Edward Howe.

"At a quarter past one o'clock on the 4th of August, I set off from Mr. Townsend's shop in State Street, with an intention of going home to dinner. Crossing the east end of the Old State House, met Mr. Selfridge, at the distance of about two rods from Townsend's shop. He passed me about three feet off on my right hand.

"I took particular notice of him, having seen the publication in the *Chronicle* that morning. He had on a frock coat, and his hands were behind him, but I am not able to say whether they were outside of his coat or not.

"I passed on six or eight steps, when I heard a very loud talking behind me. I turned immediately round, and the first thing I saw was Mr. Selfridge's hand with a pistol in it, and immediately the pistol was discharged.

"The instant afterwards, I saw the person, who had been shot, step forward from the side walk, and strike Mr. Selfridge several heavy blows on the head. These blows were struck with so much force, that I think, if Mr. Selfridge had not had on a very thick hat, they must have fractured his skull.

"He stood about three or four feet from the brick pavement or side walk, in front of Mr. Townsend's shop, and was facing up the street. I saw the Defendant throw his pistol at the deceased, but I cannot say whether it hit him or not. I saw it roll on the pavement towards Mr. Russell's door."

Another witness, Ephraim French testified:

"About one o'clock I was in Mr. Townsend's shop, and seeing old Mr. Austin go down, expected a squabble. I saw two young gentlemen go down street, and presently return. Mr. Bailey said one of them was young Mr. Austin. I saw Mr. Selfridge coming from the corner of the State House; he walked very deliberately, and looked sober.

"Young Austin went from near where I was standing, towards Mr. Selfridge. As he advanced, I saw the pistol go off, and Austin struck several severe blows, and then fell near my feet.

"I should say that the pistol, according to my observation, was one or two seconds before the first blow was struck. I did not see any cane raised before the pistol went off.

"I looked particularly at Mr. Selfridge from the time he came in sight. After he had discharged the pistol, he threw up his arms to defend his head from the blows, and afterwards threw his pistol.

"No person stood between me and the parties, so that I saw them very distinctly, having gone out of the shop and stood on the sidewalk by Mr. Townsend's shop before they met."

The actual charge was that Selfridge "in his right hand, then and there held, to, against and upon the said Charles Austin, then and there, feloniously, willfully, and of the fury of his mind, did shoot and discharge; and that he the said Thomas Oliver Selfridge, with the leaden bullet aforesaid, out of the pistol . . . did kill and slay, against the peace of the Commonwealth aforesaid, and the law in such case made and provided."

The illustrious Paul Revere was foreman of the jury, which brought a verdict of "Not Guilty," but whether or not the jury had been influenced as was claimed by "political predelictions of the jurors" will never be known. Christopher Gore, Samuel Dexter, Harrison Gray Otis, and Charles Jackson defended Thomas Oliver Selfridge, and without question did their best for "their fellow-laborer in the Federalist vineyard."

CHAPTER 9

. . . .

AMERICA'S FIRST AERIAL

PHOTOGRAPH

In an article which appeared in the August 1958 issue of *Flying,* entitled "Flashlight Lawrence," a statement is made that Lawrence, "the first aerial photographer" of America, used balloons, kites, and ingenuity when he took pictures from the air over the ruins of San Francisco after the earthquake of 1906.

The photographer may have operated as claimed, but one thing is certain—Flashlight Lawrence was *not* America's first aerial photographer.

That honor rightfully belongs to James Wallace Black, a Bostonian. In spite of this, the article in *Flying* incorrectly asserts that the San Francisco pictures, made in April 1906, were the first air photos made in this country. Actually, almost forty-six years before, on October 13, 1860, James Wallace Black took the first successful aerial picture in America from a captive balloon over Boston Common.

Mr. Black, whose earlier photographs of the construction of the present Minot's Light were masterpieces, had a studio in Boston at 173 Tremont Street, a studio in which not only did he photograph the leading citizens of the day, but taught the science of photography to Oliver Wendell Holmes and many others.

Photography in the days of the 1850s and 1860s was a very risky business, with perfect sunny weather necessary for outdoor pictures. Aerial photography was undreamed of until Black and a Providence friend, Samuel A. King, decided to attempt a picture of the Rhode Island capital from a tethered balloon high over the city.

The balloon *Queen of the Air* was used. Although at first the day was bright and clear, wind clouds were soon seen in the distance. Black, working against time while high in the air, made a hasty attempt with the wet plates then in use, and a fair picture resulted. For a brief period of time the impression remained on the sensitized glass, but before permanence could be achieved the storm clouds hit the balloon, and the fixing material spilled out and could not be applied. No more pictures could be attempted, for although the wind later diminished in strength, the clouds hid the sun for the remainder of the day. The first attempt at aerial photography had failed.

After careful organization of each minute detail of the plans, the balloon was brought to Boston. Black chose October 13, 1860, a Saturday, for the initial air photograph attempt over Boston.

The usual takeoff location on Boston Common near the baseball diamond was used, and the *Queen of the Air* soon soared aloft until it reached a position over what is now known as the Soldiers and Sailors Monument on the rise in ground then called Flagpole Hill.

There, suspended about twelve hundred feet in the air, Black ordered the curtains lowered in the basket so that he could prepare his wet plates. Pictures had to be taken almost immediately after the plates were treated with emulsion.

During the next ninety minutes he prepared and exposed

eight negatives in all. One was a great success, and it is printed in this volume. However, of the six which came out, five were blurred from the swaying of the balloon. The other two plates turned black because of the hydrogen seeping down through the neck of the gas bag and into the curtained passenger basket, ruining the wet plates at once.

Descending to earth again with his perfect picture of downtown Boston, Black loaded on fresh supplies and made ambitious plans for an untethered journey with the aid of a gentle northwesterly wind. This trip, Black hoped, would take the *Queen of the Air* down across the South Shore and relatively close to the great Minot's Ledge Lighthouse tower, of which he had already made more than a score of photographs during its construction.

The balloon started on its journey gracefully enough, as the wind was not too strong. The first picture, however, attempted over Quincy, was a failure before it could be made, for gas escaped into the basket as the aircraft climbed higher, ruining each treated plate as soon as Mr. Black finished it.

Weymouth, Hingham, and Cohasset passed below the balloonists, and still it was impossible to take any pictures because of the escaping hydrogen. Finally Scituate and the North River were below, and the balloon was eased down into a "clump of high bushes" in Marshfield, about a mile from the open sea and not too far from the site of my present Summer Street home. There had been no successful pictures of the South Shore, but the balloonists had enjoyed a thirty-mile air journey.

Returning to Boston, Black made up prints from his successful negative of the city of Boston. He found that the outer limits of the picture included the Old South Meeting House on the left, Boston Harbor at the top, Summer Street, at the right, and Winter Street at the bottom of the photograph.

There are several mysteries connected with the Black photograph. Some years ago I located in a store a sketch from the air on a glass slide of the area which apparently had been photographed by James Wallace Black that October day of 1860.

It is almost certain that the original Black photograph was copied by the artist who made the sketch or drawing. Nevertheless, a careful study of the artist's drawing reveals that there are areas in the sketch outside of the known original limits of the Black photograph. It would seem that the artist could not have indicated the correct size and shape of the various buildings from the ground as they might have appeared from the sky, so the great question is how did the artist draw the sketch which had a larger area than Black's 1860 photograph?

Possibly the original negative might have been of a larger area and, as the years went by, was gradually trimmed down by those who reproduced it. In any case the sketch is also a remarkable sky view of Boston.

Of possible interest to the reader is the first known photograph of a balloon about to take off from Boston Common in the same decade of 1860. The location is near Charles Street, and from the same area from which the *Queen of the Air* left the ground. It is definitely not the balloon from which Black made his photograph, as the letters which can be read indicate the name of the balloon in the picture was probably *Star Traveller*.

Incidentally, the 1860 newspapers were overwhelmingly enthusiastic concerning the balloon adventure and the air photograph. The Boston *Journal* described the finished picture as "forming a view at once novel and picturesque of the entire business portion of the city, and conveying an impression similar to that experienced by the aeronauts themselves."

At least two ships could be seen in the photograph. One, a steamer, was identified by Captain Edmund F. Gray as the

Eastern Queen, and by others as the *Penobscot.* It is shown at Central Wharf at the extreme left of the oval picture. The other craft is the *Romance of the Sea,* shown just below and a trifle to the left of the group a few hundred yards out from the pier.

Photographer Black realized that he had participated in an "experiment" which had "a significance far greater than that of novelty."

Oliver Wendell Holmes, noted author and poet, wrote an article for the *Atlantic Monthly* shortly afterward on photography in general, and described the Black picture of "Boston as the eagle and the wild goose sees it."

Years later, Artist Draper Hill, after studying the situation, drew an excellent sketch of the balloon landing in Marshfield.

Of course, it is possible that another person made an earlier ascent into the heavens and took a picture before October 13, 1860. However, if this was done, there is no mention of it in any known American publication, and I believe that we can safely give the credit to Mr. Black of Boston, Massachusetts, and definitely not to "Flashlight Lawrence," of California.

CHAPTER 10

• • • • • • • • • •

DOROTHY'S RESCUE

The Horse Tavern, a small "watering-place" in the woods, was located more than two centuries ago on the Stroudwater Road, leading out of Portland, Maine. An established landmark, it stood on the site of a cabin put up there in 1740 by Joe Wyer, known as "The Scout." Wyer always dressed in leather, with a powderhorn and knife slung from his shoulder, and the cabin was his lonely shelter when he was not hunting Indians.

In the summer of 1746 word reached him from Horse Beef Falls, ten miles away, that his sister Anna had been killed by the savages and her daughter Dorothy carried into captivity. Within the minute he was on the trail.

Evidently the girl had been confident of rescue, for as Wyer followed the route taken by the Indians, he noticed that Dorothy had struck her heel into the earth occasionally to leave a mark. She had also broken off twigs and leaves, and on one rock where she had rested had scattered some beads from a bracelet that Wyer had given to her on her eleventh birthday.

Wyer's trained eye was quick to see and understand these trail marks, and he followed as rapidly as he could. Once, as he slipped on a ledge, he caught a branch, tearing its foliage.

Worried that the noise had been heard by the Indians, he hid in the underbrush. A short time later an Indian came slinking back down the trail, peering cautiously about. Wyer remained motionless hardly daring to breathe. The Indian listened for some time. Then he straightened and went ahead again, evidently believing that the sound had been made by an animal of the forest and not a human.

The Indian soon caught up with his comrade, who had been walking ahead with Dorothy. Actually she had little reason to fear harm, for she guessed that she would be sold to the French in Canada. To slow up the trip as much as she could so that Wyer could catch up, she pretended to have sprained her ankle.

That night when the two savages halted they tied her wrists and ankles but then allowed her to sit beside the fire while they prepared some venison and berries for her supper. After smoking for a while, one of the Indians rolled himself in his blanket. He instantly fell asleep, leaving the other red man to watch the prisoner.

A short time later Wyer reached the scene of the night encampment. A wind was stirring in the forest, and his slow cautious steps were not heard above the swaying, creaking branches. Waiting in the shadows until the Indian had turned his head, Wyer crept up behind Dorothy and touched her shoulder. Startled, but frontier-bred, she did not give her rescuer away. Wyer quickly cut her bonds, and then, in the faintest of whispers, asked her if any other Indians were in the party. She shook her head.

Strangely enough, this headshake aroused the Indian. An instant before he had been seated stolidly on the earth with his eyes gazing out into space, but he leaped up, knife in hand. Wyer fired his rifle, and the Indian fell dead. Wyer reloaded at once.

The other Indian, awakened by the rifle shot, sprang to his

feet and attempted to get the girl away from her rescuer, but she broke and ran.

"Turn back," cried Wyer. She doubled back and started running toward him. The Indian gave up the thought of saving the girl alive, and was bent on killing them both.

Unfortunately Dorothy was now in the line of fire, so that Wyer could not use his gun for fear of hitting the girl. As the savage drew closer, he gained on Dorothy and pulled out his axe. Wyer now realized that the risk must be taken, though he might kill his niece. The Indian was a head taller than his captive, but both were in quick motion, and in spite of the moonlight, it was dark and confused under the trees. With a prayer on his lips, Wyer aimed his rifle. In the moonlight, he saw the axe lift and gleam over Dorothy's head. He fired. A lock of hair flew up—cut from his niece's head by the bullet that pierced the Indian's brain, and Dorothy ran to her rescuer.

Later as they set off on the homeward journey, they could hear wolves howling back at the campsite, as the animals quarreled over the corpses.

CHAPTER 11

• • • • • • • • • •

TALES OF NEWBURY

Every so often my thoughts return to a hike I made along the North Shore of Massachusetts more than thirty years ago. The rising hills that day were seen in the distance almost before the flat Rowley marshes with their hay staddles replaced the pastures and drumlins of Ipswich. Leaving the staddles standing as the inflowing tide surrounded them, I crossed the peaceful "prairie" of Old Newbury, and reached the foot of a long ridge of high land.

On several occasions I have lectured at the Old Newbury meetinghouse. After passing it on that particular day I reached the first of the city's several cemeteries, and walked among the graves and monuments. It was Samuel Adams Drake who wrote of the "multitude of spectators" there who are turned into stone. Looking down from my vantage point high in the cemetery I had an outstanding view of the hills of Amesbury and Salisbury, and of the Merrimac River itself, which expands into a basin enclosed with the sweep of picturesque, broken highlands. It is "here every inch a river, broad, deep, clear, and sparkling," with the city of Newburyport rising from the curved shore to the summit of the ridge, crowned with trees and steeples.

Down below the city and toward the sea all this changes.

The high shores drop into fens, marshes, and downs. A long low island thrusts itself half across the channel and blockades it. Beyond this again the sea breaks heavily on the low bar outside, with the river disappearing into a broken line of foam.

John Greenleaf Whittier has described this region. Amesbury is Whittier's home, the Merrimac his unfailing theme. Here are his surroundings:

> Stream of my fathers! sweetly still
> The sunset rays thy valley fill;
> Poured slantwise down the long defile,
> Wave, wood, and spire beneath them smile.

Newburyport is said to have been famous "for piety and privateering." Samuel Adams Drake tells us that Whittier's old schoolmaster Joshua Coffin wrote about the privateersmen of Newburyport. When putting out to sea they were accustomed to request the prayers of the churches for the success of the cruise—to which petition all those having a share in the voyage responded with a hearty amen.

Newburyport has been called a city built upon a hill. It rose and flourished through its commerce as did Salem, but when that failed, its merchants became spinners and weavers, instead of shipowners and shipbuilders.

Writing in 1883, Drake tells us how the "waterside street begins at a nest of idle shipyards, winds with the river along a line of rusty wharves, where colliers take the place of Indiamen, and ends with the antiquated suburb of Joppa,— which at least retains some of the flavor of a seaport, it having a population that gets its living by fishing, piloting, or doing such odd jobs as watermen can pick up along shore. From here the sails of a vessel that is nearing the port can be seen gliding along over the sand drifts of Plum Island or Salisbury Beach. Joppa is crowded with houses, but it is torpid.

"This long street leaves us at Oldtown, the parent settlement here, whose church spire we saw at a distance. It is narrow, irregular, and untidy; but High Street, the avenue laid out along the top of the ridge, and extending from Oldtown Green to the Chain Bridge over the Merrimack, is a thoroughfare one does not often see equalled, even if he has travelled far and seen much.

"Here, upon the cool brown of the ridge, are the stately homes of the wealthy citizens; here the old merchants, who amassed fortunes in West India rum and sugar in little stuffy countingrooms on the wharves below, lived like princes in the great roomy mansions whose windows overlooked all the town, the silvery course of the river, and the surrounding country for miles up and down.

"Although they are now sadly out of date, and of such size as to suggest that a blow of the hospitable knocker would fill them with echoes, there is an air of gentility and of good living about all these houses which makes us feel regret for the generation whose open handed hospitality has passed into a tradition; while the mansions themselves, grown venerable, continue to unite two wholly dissimilar eras.

"Usually there was an observatory on the roof, from which the owner could sweep the offing with his glass of a morning, and could run over in his mind the chance of a voyage long before his vessel had wallowed over the bar outside. He might then descend, take his cocked hat and cane from the hall table, order dinner, with an extra cover for his captain, pull out his shirt frill and go down to his counting house without a wrinkle on his brow or a crease in his silk stockings; everybody would know that his ship had come in.

"Sound in head and stomach, bluff of speech, yet with a certain homely dignity always distinguishing his class, the merchant of the olden time, undoubted autocrat to his immediate circle of dependents, was a man whose like we shall not look upon again. He left no successors."

A swarm of privateers, as well as some of the most famous vessels of the old, invincible navy, were launched here in Newburyport. In 1812 the city suffered a long blockade from the enemy's cruisers, as it was just beginning to recover from Mr. Jefferson's embargo. It was not a sinful thing in those days for the clergy to pray that a change of rulers might remove the embargo, or that a stiff gale of wind would raise the blockade—the wisdom of an overruling Providence was in control.

In the 1880s there were but two things in Newburyport for which the stranger asked. One was the tomb of George Whitefield, and the other was the mansion of Lord Timothy Dexter.

It would be difficult to think of two men whose lives were further apart. Truly, in their careers one was sublime and the other ridiculous.

Three generations ago the number of pilgrims who visited the tomb of Whitefield was amazingly large. Buried in a vault, the remains of the preacher were to be visited by entering a door underneath the pulpit of the Old South Presbyterian meetinghouse, in Federal Street. The slender and modest spire of the church, with its brazen weathercock, rose above a neighborhood quite in keeping with its own severe simplicity. Some residents claim that neither belongs to the present.

George Whitefield was born on December 16, 1713, at the Bell Inn, Gloucester, England. Choosing a preaching career, he left his homeland to spread the gospel in America. In 1769 he returned to America for the seventh and last time. He died on September 30, 1770, at Newburyport. Wesley wrote of him that Whitefield was "fairly worn out in his Master's service, as he would often preach sixty hours a week."

Let us again call on Drake:

"The house has the date 1756 over the entrance door, and is built of wood. At the left of the pulpit, as we enter, is a marble cenotaph erected to the memory of Whitefield, one face of which bears a long eulogistic inscription.

"Descending into the crypt, whose sepulchral darkness a lamp dimly lights, we are alone with its silent inmates. Yonder dark object presently shapes itself into a bier. We approach it. The coffin lid is thrown open, so as to expose what is left of its tenant,—the fleshless skull and bones of George White-field. It is not forbidden to shudder. Who, indeed, that looks can believe that 'there, Whitefield, pealed thy voice'?

"Owing, doubtless, to the fact that many come to gratify an idle curiosity, the trustees had closed the tomb 'for a spell,' as the old sexton remarked, with too evident vexation for the loss of his fees for showing it to visitors. It is a curious instance of vandalism that one of the armbones should have been surreptitiously taken from the coffin, and after having twice crossed the ocean, have found its way back to its original resting place.

"The story goes that an ardent admirer of the eloquent preacher, who wished to obtain some relic of him, gave a commission to a friend for the purpose, and this friend, it is supposed, procured the limb through the connivance of the sexton's son.

"The act of desecration being, however, discovered, aroused so much indignation everywhere, that the possessor thought it best to relinquish his prize; and he accordingly intrusted it to a shipmaster, with the injunction to see it again safely placed in the vault with his own eyes,—which direction was strictly carried out. 'And I,' finished the sexton, 'have been down in the tomb with the captain who brought that ar' bone back.' But this all happened many years ago."

This neighborhood is also the birthplace of William Lloyd Garrison, whose dwelling was the first house on the left in School Street, while the next was that in which Whitefield died of an attack of asthma.

The extraordinary religious awakening that followed Whitefield's preaching is one of the traditions common to all our New England seaboard towns.

Whitefield crossed the ocean fourteen times. He was an evangelist who preached more than eighteen thousand sermons. Whitefield's audiences were so numerous that he was often compelled to hold his meetings in the open air. When he first attempted to preach in the Newburyport area he was attacked and stoned. Strangely enough, his remains now lie in the very community where this action occurred.

Earlier in this chapter I quoted from the gifted pen of John Greenleaf Whittier. I now call on Harriet Prescott Spofford for an excerpt from her poem on the area, which takes our thoughts back to the sea:

We floated in the idle breeze,
　With all our sails a-shiver:
The shining tide came softly through,
　And filled Plum Island River.

PART THREE

. . . .

Legends

CHAPTER 1

· · · · · · · · · ·

THE RIP VAN WINKLE

OF THE BLUE HILLS

Sailors when twenty miles out to sea in Boston Bay often sight the Blue Hills of Milton. For centuries the Indians of the area gathered in the hillside vicinity.

Massachusetts Mount, as Captain John Smith called it, is said in folklore to have been one of the dead ice monsters that crawled down from the north with "stones on its back." Legend insists that all of these creatures were stopped when they reached the hollows dug by the sun god, the hollows which have become the beautiful New England lakes. There the gods pelted them with heated spears, and the glacial stones remained.

Big Blue, as it called today, now has the Harvard Observatory at its peak to identify it. Three centuries ago it was relatively unpopulated, although at its base lived the Aberginians, a tribe said to be distantly related to the Indians on the Isle of Manhattan.

The chief of the Aberginians was Wabanowi, who "thought more of himself than all the rest of the people did." He doubled in brass as a medicine man, and he was a mighty poor one. Before long, as his prophesies never came true, he was called "Headman Stick in the Mud." The chief's daughter, Heart Stealer, was as beautiful as her father was stupid. The chief made it a point to nag her and to forbid her every wish, as he thought chieftains should do.

Then came the day when Fighting Bear, chief of the Narragansetts, visited Big Blue Hill and fell in love with the girl. There he gave a long speech to Wabanowi.

In his talk he likened himself to the sun, the storm, the ocean, and to all the strong animals he could recall, while in his comments on Heart Stealer he compared her to a deer, a singing bird, a zephyr, the waves of the sea, and flowers of the field.

Then, getting down to business, Fighting Bear asked for her hand in marriage. He went on in his speech, talking of the prophecy that a great race with "sick faces, hair on its teeth, thickly clad in summer, and speaking with a harsh tongue" was soon going to drive the red man from the New England area. By this time, of course, the Indians knew that the whites had been living on the fringe of the great ocean not too far from Big Blue, but they hadn't caused trouble.

Stick-in-the-Mud, who considered himself the only prophet of the area, was outraged. Springing to his feet, he cried out:

"Who has foretold this? I didn't. There is only one prophet in this district. I am the one. It isn't for green youngsters, Narragansetts at that, to meddle with this second-sight business. Understand? Moreover, my arm is so strong it needs no help to exterminate an enemy. I can beat him with my left hand tied behind me. Had Fighting Bear merely asked for my daughter, I would have given her up without a struggle. If somebody doesn't take her soon, I shall lose my reason. But Fighting Bear has added insult to oratory, and if he doesn't leave soon, he'll never get there at all."

Thus speaking, Stick-in-the-Mud wrapped his furs around himself so that only his nose showed out.

Fighting Bear folded his arms, and with a scowl stated that his time would come. He then strode into the forest.

One evening not too long after this a heavy smoke developed over the Blue Hills, and shadowy forms were noticed flitting in and out of the smoke. All of the Indians now began to wonder what was going to happen.

Stick-in-the-Mud, who had been dozing as the smoke developed, awakened to find the spirit of a woman standing in the entrance to his wigwam. She beckoned for him to follow her, and he did so at once, hoping to discover some secret which would be more useful to him than what he considered his fortunetelling matches, which usually ended in failure.

She quickly led him up a path of the Big Blue Hill, and he followed as rapidly as he could. Finally they reached an outcropping of rock, and there was a cavern which the Indian had never noticed before, although he had walked in the area on many occasions.

The cavern glowed with a weird light, and Stick-in-the-Mud noticed that it was bedded with a soft moss. He sank without knowing why on the bed of moss, and watched entranced as the spirit began moving her arms in a slow, rotating motion. Soon he was sound asleep.

When on the next day his followers could not find him, they began searching the woods of the Blue Hill area but were unsuccessful. When the days turned into weeks and then months, his followers decided that he was not coming back, and elected another to take his place.

Down in Rhode Island, Fighting Bear heard that his tormentor had disappeared, and returned to the Blue Hills where he again claimed Heart Stealer as his future bride.

There was no one to object, and he took her back to the Providence area, where they were married.

As Charles M. Skinner tells us, now came the "men of sick

and hairy faces, white men," who desired the earth and took it, making it no longer a place pleasant to live on.

When war broke out, Fighting Bear and the other Indians fought valiantly, but lost, and decided to keep the peace in the future.

Stick-in-the-Mud, back at the cave in the Blue Hills, awakened one day to find the cavern illuminated again, with the spirit which had taken him there standing over him. Noticing that he had awakened, she spoke.

"Wabanowi, I caused you to sleep that you might be spared the pain of seeing your people forsake their home for other lands. The men with pale faces and black hearts are here. Had you been here you would have stirred them to combat and all would have perished. They did not fight. Now I set you free. Go into the Narragansett country and live with your daughter, who married Fighting Bear. Do not disturb their happiness."

The rock then swung open, and the chief staggered out into the brilliant sunshine. Full of rheumatism, this Indian Rip Van Winkle was fringed with moth-eaten whiskers which made the dogs in the area bark at him. Actually, fourteen years had elapsed.

Stick-in-the-Mud looked down into the Neponset Valley, but all his followers had gone, for there wasn't a single Indian wigwam or home in sight!

Where his village had been there were log houses and huts, and barnyard sounds were coming up to him. A horse whinnied, a rooster crowed, a sheep bleated, and a cow lowed.

After gaining a little confidence, he descended from Big Blue and reached the Neponset River, where he shaved himself as best he could with a shell. An hour later he was on the road to Providence, which he reached the next morning.

He found the home of his daughter and Fighting Bear. There were several of his grandchildren around, and they soon began playing games with him, in the most popular of which he served as a horse for the youngsters.

As the long Rip Van Winkle-like slumber had rested him, he lived many years afterward. There are those who claim that he comes back once every summer to the Blue Hills area.

Every September, on the day nearest to a full moon, he appears at Big Blue and looks off at the sunset. You may see him then, or you may see him half an hour later skimming the surface of the Neponset River in his shadow canoe. Having thus revisited the scenes of his youth, he retires for another year.

CHAPTER 2

. . . .

THE WALKING CORPSE OF MALDEN

Many of the cemeteries of New England contain graves of those whose lives are closely interwoven with the sea. There is the Medford grave of Alice, who pined away for her lost lover Faustino after his death in the sea off Nahant; the Dedham stone of Captain Williams, who was swallowed up in the ocean off Shag Rocks; and the marker in the Cape Porpoise graveyard to Captain Leander Foss, whose bark *Isidore* was lost with all on board near Cape Neddick after the disaster had been foretold in a dream.

The old graveyard of Malden, Massachusetts, however, is the burial place of Ephraim Graves whose career had nothing to do with ships and the sea. Moody and misunderstood in his life, Graves had given his nights to the study of strange mystical ideas. Chemical odors had often emanated from his house, the fumes descending into the street to cause those passing by to choke and cough. Unaccountable, mystifying noises had been heard in his laboratory, as though Graves were concocting devilish potions. Those who walked by his house at night had observed fanciful, frightening shadows flitting across his curtains. Two people who saw them fainted, and when the victims were brought back to consciousness, they were seized with terrible convulsions from which they did not fully recover for weeks.

Finally, when Graves was on his deathbed he called to his servant, who had served his master faithfully, having braved the terrors of the Malden mansion for more than sixteen years.

"Come closer," Graves gasped. "In my life I have differed from other men, and by the Devil I will continue after I am dead. My flesh is not common flesh like yours. You may not believe my claim, but my body will never rot."

Nor did it. After appropriate funeral services, at which time a strange Mephistophelean character was seen lurking in the background, the body of Ephraim Graves was put into one of the old-fashioned tombs at the Malden graveyard. Five feet below the ground, the vault was reached by an iron door in a granite gable.

The unusual assertion of Ephraim Graves was often discussed by the citizens of Malden. Twenty years after his death a group became so engrossed in his claim that the members decided to open the tomb and examine Graves' remains. When they pried open the vault, the investigators found that the corpse was almost as it had been in life, with the exception that it had grown brown and hard, and was truly dreadful to behold. Although in life Graves had not been an attractive man, apparently after death he had changed into a hideous, devilish caricature of the being they recalled.

A medical student was called from Harvard College to study the body. After his examination he announced that he was in doubt as to whether Graves' remains were in actuality still human. He had visited the cemetery alone on a squally night. Entering the tomb, he lit a lantern he had brought, after which he suspended it from a hook in the vault. Then, with some composure, he sawed the head of Graves from the body and put it into a bag, intending to remove it to his home, where he could examine it at leisure. It took more than an hour to complete this awesome business, and before he finished his work he began to hear whispers of protest coming from other coffins in the sepulcher. Then he was troubled by footfalls sounding on the walk outside, moans, wails, and stifled cries. At regular intervals he would hear groans, followed by pitiful screams of what apparently were lost souls.

A moment later he noticed shadows forming on the green, slimy wall of the tomb, shadows which began to take form and leave the wall. With a yell for mercy, the Harvard student flung the head of Ephraim Graves upon the vault floor, leaped out of the pit, and ran at remarkable speed toward the cemetery gate, crashing into tombs and overturning gravestones in his frantic efforts to escape. Reaching the University, he never returned to the Malden cemetery for further research.

There were others, however, who appeared interested in additional exploration of the vault. Several months later a medium from upper New York claimed he had been delegated by two clairvoyants, the Fox sisters, to investigate the remains of Ephraim Graves. The medium visited the tomb, examined the severed head and the remainder of the body, but departed from Malden without ever making his findings known.

As a chronicler of the period records, "curiosity would not be stayed," and it became the custom for adventuresome boys to go into the tomb and pick up the severed head from time to time. Unfortunately, in this manner the skull was bound to vanish eventually, and it did.

Before it disappeared, quite often the boys would hold up the head at the door of the tomb to scare their friends, especially the girls. This was always in the daytime, with a bright sun shining, as, of course, nobody in Malden would enter the graveyard after dark.

It became known that, in the night at the stroke of twelve, the iron tomb door would fly open. Indeed, few Malden residents dared be caught there to see the fearful thing happen. On the last stroke of the bell the tomb door would swing ajar. Then the horrific, gruesome remains of Ephraim Graves in its mildewed garments would crawl out of the coffin. Pulling itself up by the door ledge, it began to stalk about the cemetery as if in search of its head. At the first sign of daylight, it went back to rest.

About a century and a half ago a man bathing in the nearby river just before sunrise saw a white-robed figure scramble out of Graves' tomb. Too terrified to realize what he was doing, the bather fled through the Malden streets, naked as he was, waking the residents of many of the houses with his frightened cries. It was found that the figure actually was not a corpse but a poor, insane creature who had crawled into the house of death to sleep. The bather was so upset that he refused to believe the explanation. Insisting that he had been summoned by a ghost, from that very day he began to change. He became silent and self-absorbed, and wasted slowly away. His death occurred shortly afterward.

The authorities now decided to bury the tomb forever, and ordered workmen to dump cartloads of earth upon it until the entire gable was buried. The corpse was never afterward seen abroad in the Malden area.

Today only a slightly flattened mound marks the tomb, completely underground, where Ephraim Graves was interred so many years ago.

CHAPTER 3

. . . .

THE OLD MAN OF THE MOUNTAINS

Folklore involving the Old Man of the Mountains originally concerned only the Indians, but when Nathaniel Hawthorne changed all this in his story of *The Great Stone Face,*
the older tale was put into the background. Nevertheless, the
old Indian legend is still worth telling.

For many centuries the Pennacook tribe of Indians lived
in the White Mountains. After the venerable Passaconaway
had been transferred to heaven on his fire-car, the position
of chief fell to his son, Wonalonset. His rule for some years
was happy, his people trusted him, and he found a helpful
wife in Mineola, daughter of Chocorua.

Unfortunately, trouble came in time, as it does to all na-
tions and all peoples. When Indian Princess Rimmon, Mineola's sister, discovered that she was in love with Wonalonset,
she made certain exploratory gestures in his direction. Finding that all her efforts were in vain, and that Chief Wonalonset was happy and content in his family relationship and actually not aware of her longing, she climbed a steep cliff to the
west of Amoskeag Falls, and leaped to her death.

Although historians claim that most Lover's Leap stories
are fictitious, there is another account that concerns the
Squantum cliffs in Boston Harbor. Benjamin Lynde, a former

owner of nearby Thompson's Island who died in 1767, wrote
the story in poetry.

> Close, on the south, a Cliff lifts up its brow,
> High, prominent o'er the parting stream below,
> From whence the Native's fate-predicting squaw
> Their ruin, and the Briton's Rise foresaw;
> That Heaven's swift plagues shall quickly sweep away
> The Indians 'round the Massachusetts Bay.
> But she (while they her rage prophetic mock)
> Flings headlong down from the steep craggy rock;
> Mu-Squantum! from her dying murmurs fell,
> And thence call'd Squantum Neck, (as ancients tell).

Up in the White Mountains Wonalonset never knew the
reason for Rimmon's suicide, but almost at once the Pennacooks' fortunes changed. They had lived in a peace their
watchful enemies said was weakness, and their chief had become a praying Indian. Shortly after Rimmon's death a young
Mohawk chief named Konassaden began to rake up some forgotten injuries. He stirred up his people to remember and
revenge. He cried out that Passaconaway, who commanded
the spirits, was no longer to be feared, if he could raise five
hundred men to overcome the Pennacooks. Konassaden
picked his best and bravest warriors and left his home in the
Adirondacks for the White Mountain land of the Agiochooks,
his allies.

Later, he arrived at the camp of Wonalonset's people while
only the women, children, and aged were there, the hunters
having departed on an expedition in search of fish and game.
When the hunters returned they found only burned ruins of
their homes with the corpses of their fathers lying among the
ashes. As the trail was still fresh they lost no time in pursuing
the Mohawks, who had taken all the women and children.

Coming upon the fleeing Indians and their captives, they

fought for the recovery of their loved ones, but the Mohawks fled and were lost among the ghostly and forbidden mountains of Franconia.

It is said that in the last hours of their flight, they were led by a tall, dark man, a tireless man with legs of oak, who kept so far ahead that they could not be sure it was Konassaden, yet nobody had seen Konassaden fall out. On through tangled woods they went, "heavy with sleep, empty of food." Some of the Mohawks were seriously wounded, and could only keep up by superhuman efforts.

On they went, over slippery ledges covered with moss, under windfalls which led to broken masses of granite, until finally the peaks of the Agiochooks were against the stars before them. Discovering a valley, they stumbled into it with exhaustion. Finding a stream, they drank from it, after which they stretched out on the grass and fell asleep.

In the morning they arose and looked for their leader, Konassaden. An exclamation of astonishment and awe caused every eye to turn aloft. From the crest of a mighty cliff which the sunrise was illuminating they saw, wreathed in a cloud, the mighty, solemn face of stone.

"It is the Great Spirit!" cried the Mohawks. Falling on their faces, they looked again, but the morning glow had already faded and the giant face was dark and stern. Suddenly a blaze of light filled the valley for an instant. The Indians sprang to their feet, and a voice spoke in thunderous tones.

"You have warred needlessly on your brothers. You have invaded the hills which are the home of Manitou.* You have neglected your wives and children to shed human blood. I am angered at your cruelty. Therefore, die. But you shall be a warning in your deaths. You shall be turned to rocks on this mountain-side."

---

* Manitou was the traditional Great Spirit of the Indians.

One by one, the Mohawks then sank down to the earth in a deep sleep from which they never awakened. As was predicted, their bodies turned into giant boulders which still can be seen at the foot of the stone Manitou's throne.

CHAPTER 4

· · · · · · · · · ·

THE DEVIL IN CONNECTICUT

In my *Legends of the New England Coast* I tell the story of the Devil and Jonathan Moulton. The scene is Hampton, New Hampshire. In this story, however, we go to Connecticut and across to Springfield, Massachusetts, for the account of Parson Elbridge Hooker.

We are informed that you must never lose your wits when the Devil is about, as Mephistopheles is unceasing in his devices for the upsetting of good morals. There is the story of the four lads in a Connecticut village, for instance, who knew well enough that card-playing was a sin, but intended to make it merely a little sin one Saturday night by playing for only a few minutes. A stump of a candle was on the table when they began, and they lighted it, saying, "We will stop as soon as the candle goes out." They played and played. Looking up after a time they discovered that it was daybreak and that they had been at the cards all Saturday night. Of course the Devil had kept the candle burning, and it is dreadful to think what happened in consequence.

This instance and others like it were doubtless known to good, keen Parson Hooker, and he profited by his meditations on them, as will be shown.

His church affairs often brought him to locations far from home. Traveling on horseback, at one time he found himself late in the afternoon at the village of Springfield, Massachusetts, where he put up at the inn. There were so many people in the house that the best the landlord could suggest was the so-called haunted room.

Unknown to the preacher, there wasn't a single resident of Springfield who would dare to stay in the room overnight. Nevertheless it proved to be a comfortable, well-furnished apartment.

After dutifully reading a chapter in his Bible, the minister went to bed. At midnight he was aroused by a commotion and found his bed surrounded by witches.

It seems as if all the hags from Salem and many other witch-ridden settlements were crowding into his room. They arrived by the chimney, they came in at the open window, and those who could squeezed through the crack under the door. Presently they set a "noble feast" on a table with gold and silver dishes. Then, as the fiends of the Devil were about to sit down for a joyous repast, they realized that Parson Hooker, whose eyes bulged like dark lanterns over a rim of bedclothes, was in the room. Clamoring with delight, they suggested that he draw up a chair and eat with them.

The parson had supped but lightly, and he was tempted. Nevertheless, it was known that if one ate with witches, he could easily become a witch himself. After a moment of thought he decided to join the witches but would do his best to reform them. He arose, slipped on his breeches, and sat with the rabble of uncouth creatures at the table.

"It is my habit," announced the parson, "to ask a blessing on my meals." At the first words of the prayer the creatures fled, muttering and sputtering, leaving everything to the clergyman, who ate a good meal and put the gold and silver plate into his saddlebags.

As he rode away in the morning a crow squawked from a tree overhead, "You're Hooker by name, hooker by nature, and you've hooked it all."

CHAPTER 5

. . . .

GRINDSTONE HILL

The Penobscot River, in its twenty-four-mile stretch from Bangor to the sea, has many twists and turns which have always fascinated me. Those twists and turns at one time were crowded with more lumber vessels than any other locations in the world!

Near the west branch of the Penobscot is a tall hill, shaped in the form of a grindstone, on edge and half sunk in the ground. The oddity of Grindstone Hill has given rise to many queer tales, and as is often the case, much folklore exists concerning its origin. The Indian legend which follows goes back several hundred years.

Long before the white people crossed the Atlantic to bother the red people, a little yellow moon was often seen floating through the heavens in the wake of the larger one that is still shining. Melgasoway was an Indian lad who was like many boys of today. He would rather practice with his bows and arrows and worry the dogs and go fishing and swimming and climb trees and pick berries than gather firewood and do errands.

One day his mother sent him to fetch a pumpkin out of a cornfield for supper. No doubt Melgasoway intended to gather the fruit and dutifully return with it. Unfortunately he saw a rabbit and chased it so long that when the sun set he found himself miles from home and very tired and hungry. The big moon set soon after the sun, so that the boy would not have been back until morning had it not been for the little moon's light. As this tiny orb lifted into view he stood still and laughed aloud.

Seen through the branches, the tiny moon looked like a pumpkin. Melgasoway did not dare to go back without the pumpkin, but the cornfield was a mile or so out of his way. His mother was old and nearsighted, and this tiny moon might pass for a pumpkin if only he could bring it down. As it came swinging above him he drew his arrow to the head and shot. The shaft passed out of his sight and he thought he had missed his mark, but within a short time the moon began to quiver, then pitch out of the sky and tumble toward the earth. Now it had been supposed that this little moon was just above the treetops and was no larger than a pumpkin. Great was the astonishment of Melgasoway when it grew and grew in his sight until he saw that he would be crushed if he stayed there any longer. And, as the legend goes, he moved away rapidly.

Melgasoway ran off to get his spanking at home, yelling with dismay, for while the falling mass was still some distance from the earth he saw that hundreds of devils were clinging to it; yellow devils with long tails and claws. Melgasoway took his whipping with positive enjoyment, for he expected worse, now that he had destroyed a moon and released a company of imps into the woods. Yet he told his people what he had done, and they, who had met the devils already in the neighborhood and had discovered the moon stuck in the swamp with its light out, praised him for his daring and made him medicine man. So Melgasoway lived to the end of his days in sight of the hill on the Penobscot River which he had brought down from the sky.

The Yankee version is that the hill was put where it is by a wizard in order to accommodate the mowers at opposite ends of the nearby hayfield when they might need to sharpen their scythes. The Grindstone Hill was supposed to be turned by means of a water wheel in the west branch.

There is an Irish version which says that the hill is the wheel of a barrow on which a stout fellow was trundling a monument back to the North Pole where his ancestors had placed it. The monument had floated down to Maine on an iceberg.

A French woodsman, who, up to the turn of the century, came down to chop wood and return to Canada at the end of the lumbering season, knew Grindstone Hill and often told his version of how it came there. During the war which ended French rule in Canada a number of Frenchmen were marching across Maine to join Montcalm's garrison in Quebec. It was August, and one afternoon the heat and thunderstorms were trying the temper of the men. It was raining especially hard, and every man of the dripping, bedraggled party had exhausted himself in swearing.

The captain, one Antoine LeBlanc, roared out a compound oath in two languages that nearly loosened his molars, shouting that he wished it would rain grindstones and harrow-teeth and have done with it.

Hardly had he uttered this wish and coupled it with an invocation to the Devil ere a dense shadow fell upon the spot and a fearful rushing sound was heard. Then, plunging through the clouds, came this father of all grindstones, and, tumbling on the company, buried them in mud—all but the man who survived to tell what happened, and this he would not have done but for being so frightened at the oaths that his legs were weak and he could not keep up with his comrades.

The Penobscot River today is not the active waterway of the old days, but the summer visitors drive up and down the river and cross the bridges, few having heard of Grindstone Hill.

CHAPTER 6

. . . .

UNUSUAL CREATURES OF THE

MAINE WOODS

Charles M. Skinner, who visited the Maine woods in the 1890s, collected many stories of unusual creatures of folklore, such as the will-am-alone, the side-hill-winder, and the dingball.

He feared that some of the creatures which infest the woods of the lumbering counties of Aroostock, Piscataquis, and Penobscot have had their unusual qualities magnified in local myths for the silencing of fretful children and the stimulation of generosity on the part of green wood choppers.

It is the newcomer in a lumber camp who is subjected to the usual amount of hazing, just as he might be as a freshman in college, and he is expected to do a little more than his share of the breakfast getting, errand running, and the like in order to quiet the hostility of the will-am-alones. Today, it is said, these creatures are not seen as often as they were, for they have a fixed hostility to mankind and educational institutions, never venturing within ten miles of a school.

The will-am-alone is a quick little animal, resembling a squirrel, that rolls poisonous lichens in its fingers and drops them into the ears and on the eyelids of sleeping men in

camp, causing them to have strange dreams, rashes, and head-
aches, and to see unusual, unbelievable objects in the snow.
Quite often the hardest drinkers in the camp are said to be
most easily and most often affected by the poison.

The side-hill-winder is a rabbitlike creature so called because he winds about steep hills in only one direction. Because of this, in order that his back may be kept level, the
down-hill legs are longer than the up-hill pair. He is seldom
caught but this can be done by heading him off with dogs
when he is corkscrewing up a mountain. As the dogs slowly
turn the winder, his long legs come on the up-hill side and
tip him over. He is then an easy prey to the canine creatures
chasing him.

Much to be dreaded is the dingball, a panther whose last
tail joint is not only bare of flesh but ball-shaped, resembling
a four-pound shot. With this weapon it cracks its victim's
skull, and there is no record of a survival from the blow of a
dingball. In more ancient times it is said to have sung with
a human voice, and in this way lured unsuspecting humans
from their cabins to have their heads broken in the dark. The
dingball is fond of mankind and will sing all night for a meal
of white human flesh.

Stay away from razorshins, a deathless red man who works
for such as are kind to him, but mutilates those who neglect
to pay tribute in alcohol. The trick is to keep razorshins supplied with firewater, a jug at every full moon, and he will
very often fell a tree for you with his sharp shinbones, or, if
nobody is around, will clear up a bit of road. But if you begin
to omit his monthly stimulation, you must be prepared for
the possibility of losing your scalp, which this Indian can
slice from your head with a single kick. He is also proficient
in clipping ears and is capable of leaving cuts that will look
like saber strokes. When a green hand arrives in a lumber
camp it is his duty to slake the thirst of razorshins. He puts

a jug of virulent Bangor whiskey at the door. The best proof that he exists is the unusual odor which pervades the premises all night and the empty jug which is discovered in the morning.

At the turn of the present century, when French Canadian lumbermen were chopping down the trees, the men would quit work if a white owl flew from any tree they were felling. Not one of them would look back or shout at it, for it was a ghost and would cause them much trouble unless they left that part of the wood for thirty days.

The windigo, a being in human form, is said to be the worst woods creature of all, but is seen only in the sparsely populated areas of Maine and the thickest wooded districts. A Canadian Indian is the only man who ever saw one and lived, but why no one knows. Merely to look upon the windigo is doom, and even to cross his track is deadly peril. His footprints are twenty-four inches long, and in the middle of each imprint is a red spot, showing where his blood has oozed through a hole in his moccasin.

Dark, huge, and shadowy as he seems, the windigo still has a human shape and many human characteristics. Strangely enough the belief in this monster is still said to be so genuine that lumbermen on occasion secure a monopoly of certain jobs by scaring competitors out of the neighborhood. Those in the know say that the simple device of tramping past rival camps in fur-covered snowshoes and squeezing a drop of beef blood or paint into each footprint usually is enough. One particularly effective episode caused the flight of Indian choppers from a lumber district, and no one could persuade them to return to work, for the windigo's track had been seen. It was claimed that this particular windigo was an Irishman who was not a bad fellow at all, but the Indians would not be convinced, and kept away for the rest of the season. Indeed, it is said that the "stealthy stride" of the windigo monster makes every lumberman's blood run cold, and his mere mention is to be avoided.

A devil named Pomoola lives on the slopes of Mount Katahdin in Maine. This devil, a being that has the shape of a panther but is larger and wears four tusks that hang out of his mouth for fourteen inches, will gladly eat animals and Indians, but on the other hand is so terrified by white men that no scientist has been able to see him, even with strong binoculars. Bullets are powerless against him, while knives mean nothing. He is vulnerable only to a stroke of lightning, which can kill him.

Before the first white man came to the Maine forests Pomoola made a yearly levy on the Indians, selecting half a dozen annually, but since the advent of Europeans the male Indians have become so "flavored with rum" that Pomoola can stomach only the maidens.

In the year 1823 Pomoola killed four members of a large hunting party on Jo Mary Lake, three more the next day at South Turn Lake, and was on the verge of overtaking the survivors at Millinocket Rips, near Elbow Lake, when a thunderstorm hit the area. Pomoola, so the legend goes, was struck and killed by lightning during the storm. The Indians say that when found he was measured and his length was twice as long as a four-man canoe. The body was floated to Old Town on two boats, and the people of that Indian reservation capital celebrated the death of Pomoola with candles and firewater.

One of the tusks, blackened by the lightning, is treasured in the family of the descendants of old Chief Sockalexis. Geologists have seen it and say it came out of the head of the saber-toothed tiger that lived in the Maine woods several millions of years ago. As writer Charles M. Skinner said in 1903, scientists did not live in Maine in 1823, so how could they possibly know that the tiger did not hold over until that date?

CHAPTER 7

· · · · · · · · · ·

PETER RUGG, THE MISSING MAN

Peter Rugg originally was mentioned by William Austin in a letter supposedly written by Jonathan Dunwell of New York to Herman Krauff.

In the summer of 1820 Jonathan Dunwell of New York was on a stagecoach going from Providence to Boston, riding up front with the driver. Reaching Attleboro, Massachusetts, Dunwell noticed that the horses "suddenly threw their ears back on their necks as flat as a hare's."

The driver explained that the storm breeder was coming. Soon afterward a small speck was sighted far ahead on the road which is now known as Route One. A few minutes later an open makeshift chaise drawn by a large black horse came rolling toward them at about twelve miles an hour. The driver, a small child at his side, was grasping the reins with "firmness." His appearance was one of dejection, and he glanced anxiously at the stage passengers and driver as he went by. Horse and chaise were soon out of sight, vanishing in the direction of Providence.

A moment later Dunwell noticed that the horses' ears were back in place, and all seemed normal again. He asked the driver about the man, and the driver explained that although no one really knew him or the small girl at his side, he had

145

met the chaise "more than a hundred times." The stage driver said that the occupant of the chaise had often asked him the way to Boston, even when the carriage was heading for Providence and away from Boston. Lately, however, the man had refused to talk with him. The driver was sure of one thing—that a rainstorm always followed an encounter with the chaise.

Sometime later the coach ascended a "high hill in Walpole," and Dunwell began to think that as there was not a cloud "big as a marble" in sight, the driver was wrong, and he told him so.

"So look in the direction whence the man came," answered the driver. "The storm never meets him; it follows him."

On the crest of the next hill the driver pointed out a speck of cloud the size of a hat, and then expressed a fear that their stop at Polley's Tavern could not be made before the storm hit.

"The wanderer and his child will go to Providence through rain, thunder, and lightning," concluded the driver.

Instinctively the horses began to speed up. The little black cloud came rolling down the turnpike toward them, spreading out in all directions as it approached. Successive flashes of chain lightning caused the cloud to display "a thousand fantastic images."

The driver confided that every flash of lightning near its "centre discovered to him distinctly the form of a man sitting in an open carriage drawn by a black horse." Try as he could, however, Dunwell saw no such image in the darkened sky.

Reaching Polley's Tavern, the passengers scrambled inside just as the heavens opened up, but as soon as all were inside, the torrential rain was over, almost as quickly as it had started.

A moment later a gentleman drove up and told the others that he had been stopped by the same chaise. The driver had asked the gentleman for the way to Boston, after which he had driven off in the opposite direction. Looking back, the gentleman had watched as a thunderclap broke directly over the chaise, enveloping man, child, horse and carriage.

"I stopped," said the gentleman, "supposing the lightning had struck him, but the horse seemed to loom up and increase his speed!"

A few minutes afterward a peddler with a cart stopped at the inn, everything dripping from the storm. He explained that he had met the chaise in four different states within a fortnight, and was getting fed up with the encounters. Each time the man had asked the way to Boston and each time shortly after the man had driven away, the peddler had been caught in a cloudburst. The peddler ended by saying that he was going to take out marine insurance for the future.

"In short," stated the peddler, "I wish never to see that man and horse again; they do not look to me as though they belonged to this world." The coach passengers soon climbed aboard, and traveled the remainder of the journey from Providence to Boston without further incident.

Three years later Dunwell was in Hartford, Connecticut, standing on the doorstep of Bennett's Hotel when he heard a man say something that intrigued him.

"There goes Peter Rugg and his child! He looks wet and weary, and farther from Boston than ever."

Dunwell spoke up. "Peter Rugg! And who is Peter Rugg?"

"He is a famous traveler, held in light esteem by all innholders, for he never stops to eat, drink, or sleep. I wonder why the government does not employ him to carry the mail."

"But," said Dunwell, "does the man never stop anywhere? Does he never converse with anyone? I saw the same man more than three years since near Providence, and even then I heard a strange story about him."

"Sir," said the stranger, "those who know the most respecting that man say the least. I have heard it asserted that Heaven sometimes sets a mark on a man either for a judgment or a trial. Under which Peter Rugg now labors, I cannot say, therefore I am rather inclined to pity than to judge.

"He looks as though he never ate, drank, or slept. His child looks older than himself; and he looks like time broken off from eternity, and anxious to gain a resting place.

"As for his horse, he looks fatter and gayer, and shows more animation than he did twenty years ago. The last time Rugg spoke to me he inquired how far it was to Boston. I told him just one hundred miles.

" 'Why,' he said, 'how can you deceive me so? It is cruel to mislead a traveler. I have lost my way; pray direct me to the nearest route to Boston.'

"I repeated that it was one hundred miles.

" 'How can you say so? I was told last night it was but fifty, and I have traveled all night.'

"I explained that he was going away from Boston, and of course he must turn back.

" 'Alas,' was his answer. 'It is all turn back. Boston shifts with the wind, and plays all around the compass. One man tells me it is to the east, another to the west, and as for the guide posts, they all point the wrong way.'

"He then gave the reins to the horse and they disappeared within a moment. A few days afterward I met the man in Unity, New Hampshire, a little this side of Claremont, and he was going at the rate of twelve miles an hour."

To everyone's surprise, a short time later a dark, high-spirited horse came down the road toward Bennett's Hotel. Realizing that it might be the chaise, Jonathan Dunwell stepped into the street, making a feint to stop him.

The driver reined his horse at once.

"Sir," said Dunwell, "are you not Peter Rugg?"

"My name is Peter Rugg," came the answer. "I have unfortunately lost my way. I am wet and weary, and would take it kindly if you direct me to Boston."

"You live in Boston? And in what street?"

"In Middle Street."

"How did you become wet, for it hasn't rained here today?"

"It just rained a heavy shower up the Merrimac River. But should I take the old road or the Newburyport Turnpike?"

"But this is not Newburyport, and the Merrimac River is a long distance away. This is Hartford, Connecticut."

Rugg wrung his hands and looked incredulous.

"Have the rivers, too, changed their courses, as the cities have changed places? Ah, that fatal oath!"

Peter Rugg then reined his horse, and a moment later was off, the horse's "hind flanks rising like wings."

Dunwell, having discovered a clue in Peter Rugg's history— that he had lived in Middle Street, Boston—decided that the next time he visited the Massachusetts capital he would make further inquiries. A short time later he arrived in Boston and went to the home of a Mrs. Croft in Middle Street. She told him that she had resided in Boston since 1803. Dunwell became excited when she was able to recall that Peter Rugg had actually visited her, probably in the summer of 1818. Possibly Peter Rugg had confused even himself and had doubled back to Boston that year.

Mrs. Croft explained that in answer to a knock she had opened the door to find Peter Rugg and his daughter, while nearby in the street she noticed an old weatherbeaten chaise hitched to a black horse.

"I would like to speak to my wife, Catherine Rugg," Peter had said.

"I am sorry, but Catherine Rugg has been dead for many years," came the answer, whereupon Peter Rugg became excited.

"How can you deceive me so? Do ask Catherine to step to the door."

"Sir, I assure you that Mrs. Rugg has not lived here these

many years. There is no one here but myself, and I am Betsy Croft."

Peter Rugg paused and looked up and down the street.

"Everything has changed," he remarked. "The streets have changed, the town has changed, and what is strangest of all, Catherine Rugg has deserted her husband and child. Now, Madame, will you please direct me to Boston?"

"Why," exclaimed Mrs. Croft, "this is Boston."

"Just a minute," answered Peter, "I recollect now. I came over a bridge instead of a ferry. Pray, what bridge was it?"

"It is the Charles River Bridge."

"Ah, that explains it. I perceive my mistake. There is a ferry between Boston and Charlestown; there is no bridge. Therefore I have made a mistake."

Peter Rugg and his daughter returned to the chaise, and a moment later drove away. That was the entire story as Mrs. Croft could recall it. She now suggested that Dunwell talk with a Mr. James Felt, an antiquarian. Felt, during the interview, expressed surprise when Dunwell said that he had seen Rugg and his small daughter not too long before.

"Why, my friend," admitted Felt, "that Peter Rugg is now a living man, I will not deny, but that you have seen Peter Rugg and his child is impossible, if you mean a small child, for Jenny Rugg, if living, must be at least, let me see, Boston Massacre, 1770, Jenny was about ten years old. Why, sir, Jenny Rugg must now be at least sixty years old."

Dunwell realized that he had as much information from Mr. Felt as he could get. He thanked the aged man and returned to his Marlborough Hotel room. Beginning to mull over what Mrs. Croft and James Felt had told him, he realized that if Peter Rugg had been traveling since the Boston Massacre, there wasn't any reason why he shouldn't keep on traveling to the end of time.

Later, while discussing Peter Rugg at the hotel, he met a Boston resident whose family had long lived in the town.

"Peter Rugg," said the resident, "once lived in Middle Street. He was a man in comfortable circumstances, but unhappily, his temper was at times altogether ungovernable, and his language was terrible. In these fits of passion, if a door stood in his way, he would never do less than kick a panel through."

Once Rugg was seen to bite a tenpenny nail in halves. In those days everybody, both men and boys, wore wigs. Peter, at these moments of violent passion, would become so profane that his wig would rise up from his head. Some said it was on account of his terrible language. Others were of the opinion that it was caused by the expansion of his scalp, for violence swells the veins and expands the head.

While these fits were on him Rugg had no respect for heaven or earth. Except for this weakness, all agreed that Rugg was a good sort when his fits were over.

One morning late in the autumn Rugg, in his own chaise, with a large bay horse, took his daughter and proceeded to Concord. On his return a violent storm caught up with him. At dark he stopped in Menotomy, now Arlington, at the door of Mr. Cutter, a friend of his, who urged him because of threatening weather to tarry the night. On Rugg's declining to stop, Mr. Cutter became concerned and vehemently urged him to remain.

"Why," said Cutter, "the storm is a terrible one and you should not go out again. The gale actually will overwhelm you and your daughter, who may perish! The night is very dark. You are in a open chaise, and the tempest is getting worse."

"Let the storm increase," came the answer, and then Rugg swore a fearful oath. "I will reach home tonight, in spite of the tempest's blast, or I never will reach home again at all." Rugg whipped up his horse, and a moment later horse and chaise started to disappear down the road.

Peter Rugg did not reach home that night, or the next, or the next. When his wife told the authorities that he was missing, along with his daughter, they never could trace him after he left Menotomy. For years after, on every dark and stormy night, his wife would fancy that she heard the crack of a whip, the tread of a horse, and the rattling of a chaise as it passed her home on Middle Street, Boston. The neighbors, also, heard the same noise.

One special night the neighbors decided to await the possible arrival of Peter Rugg, and lighted their lanterns to be ready for him. Surely enough, he came down Middle Street, pulled by his great horse and with his daughter at his side, and their lanterns illuminated the scene very effectively. To their amazement, the horse pulled the carriage right by Peter Rugg's door, although every neighbor watching could see the poor man strain and struggle as he tried to slow up the horse, but it was all in vain.

Wondering just where Rugg did stop, the neighbors visited every Boston inn, public house and stable, but it developed that Rugg stayed nowhere in Boston that night. The neighbors, quite shocked at the turn of events, never did try to watch again, and several of them considered what they had witnessed as no less than a delusion. Others shook their heads and said nothing.

Rugg was then reported in Connecticut, after which New Hampshire became the scene of his appearances. Then there would be talk of a man with a small child driving through Newport, followed by a storm.

His last known appearance in the Boston area was on Charlestown Bridge. The toll gatherer asserted that on occasion, usually on the darkest and stormiest nights of all, a horse and wheel carriage, with a terrible noise, would pass

over the bridge at midnight, in "utter contempt of toll rates."
Finally the toll collector decided to take action, and one
rainy night stationed himself in the very center of the bridge.
Soon he heard the noise of horse and chaise coming from
Charlestown Square.

Just as the horse and carriage passed him, he threw the
three-legged stool he had brought right at the horse, but to
his astonishment the stool passed harmlessly through the
animal, and clattered to a stop some distance away.

Peter Rugg, his horse, and his daughter were never seen
again in Boston or on any approach leading to the Massachusetts capital.

Perhaps, some day, when you are driving along a New
England road, you may see Peter Rugg and his daughter. On
the other hand, I hope not.

CHAPTER 8

· · · · · · · · · · ·

A ROLLICKING GHOST

The taverns of Massachusetts and New England have been the subject of several outstanding books, but in none of them have I read of the so-called rollicking ghost of the Bay State's Buxton Inn.

On a winter night, with harsh weather outside, "snow and wind and cold," the travelers, stormbound in the tavern, had gathered in the cozy taproom where they were playing cards and enjoying their flip, pipes, and storytelling. From time to time the singers would join in a chorus, none too steady or tuneful, but hearty and jolly.

Around midnight the knocker on the inn door gave a lively rat-tat, and, as the landlord was rheumatic and fumbled at the bolt, the first summons was followed by a couple of sound kicks.

"Let him in out o' the weather, heaven's name!" urged one.

"'Tis one more to our party, and the more the merrier," declared another.

The door finally was opened, revealing a dashing, handsome young man whose gold-laced garments, out of style to tell the truth, were covered with snow. He entered and shook the white burden to the floor with a stamp, a laugh, and an oath, and there seemed a prodigious deal of it.

"Gad, neighbor," exclaimed one of the roisterers, "you must have been buried!"

The young fellow told the landlord that his horses had been stabled, and his servant had found lodging in the loft. He had supped, but he wanted tobacco and drink, "if I have the price for them," he added, slapping his pocket, with a roguish smile. "If not, I'll throw the dice with any or all in the company."

The others were willing enough, and after several hours every penny in the pockets of the company had transferred itself to the purse of this unknown visitor who now sat, tilted in his chair sipping the last of his drink. He began to talk to his victims in insolent fashion.

Presently the old serving woman came in to begin her day's work, to put out the candles, sweep the hearth, and take the glasses to the kitchen. The storm was over and the dawn was in the east. She stared long at the young visitor, who, with pipe in mouth, was looking perhaps a trifle faded in the gray light. He stared fixedly at her.

"Master, you do be the very cut of Sir Charles, off our signboard," she cried.

"Is it so?" asked the guest. "Then let's see what I look like."

The others, startled at the old woman's discovery, followed her to the window. Surely, Captain Charles Buxton in the paint was very like this character in the flesh. Without question, indeed, one straining his eyes out of the smoky room into the morning twilight might have indulged the fancy that Sir Charles out there in the snow had put on a sneering expression overnight, and that the lid of the right eye had dropped knowingly, just a trifle. And one of the fellows said, in a voice thickened with the night's drinking, "It's the image. Dom'd if he isn't looking down at us!"

Every person in the room turned to compare the picture with the person, but the visitor had vanished. No door or window was open, there were no footprints in the snow, but the visitor had completely disappeared. Although he was never seen again, many who later studied the signboard firmly believed that from the night of the storm Sir Charles had indeed taken on a different outlook as he swung back and forth at the door of the inn which was named for him.

CHAPTER 9

. . . .

CORONATION ROCK

Coronation Rock, in Charlestown, Rhode Island, was from time immemorial the place where the Narragansett Indians crowned their chieftains. The last such event was in 1770, as the date inscribed on the rock attests.

According to Tom Rogers, who came from Nantucket, the area around the rock was also a region of demons and sprites for many years. Rogers was so afraid of the Coronation Rock spirits of the other world that he would often go far out of his way at night to avoid passing in the vicinity of ghosts or goblins.

One night, however, there was a husking bee of great magnitude two miles from his house, and he "kept his spirits up by pouring spirits down." By the time the dance ended he had sufficient false courage to walk right by Coronation Rock, and this he started out to do.

Approaching the rock, he noticed a glow in the trees, and then he heard the sound of a fiddle, going "like mad." Pushing his way through a thicket, he soon heard the shuffle of feet. A minute later he was at the rock itself, and such a sight it was, a sight he had never seen before. Extremely anxious to shake a leg in a jig or reel, he could not miss a chance like this.

Entering the clearing, all smiles, he was welcomed with a shout. On a mossy hummock sat a maid without a partner, a maid whose black eyes snapped with mischief and whose cheeks and lips were rosy. Tom caught her by the waist, dragged her to her feet, and whirled off with her into the gayest, wildest dance he had ever led. He actually seemed to soar above the earth, and after a time Tom found that the others had seated themselves and were watching him and the maid.

This put him on his mettle, and the violin soon gave lightning to his heels. Then he and the girl separated for a matter of six feet and set in to dance each other down. As he leaped and whirled and cracked his heels in the air in an ecstasy of motion Tom noticed that the freshness was leaving his partner's face. Her features were becoming longer, the eyes deeper and harder. He was dismayed when he saw that the eyes had turned green and evil, the teeth began to project, sharp and yellow, below the lip, and her form had grown lank and withered. He realized with a shock that it was the demon crew of the hill with which he was in company, and his heart grew heavy. Now he could barely leap, yet leap he must, for he was lost to the forces of evil unless he could keep up the dance until sunrise or unless a clergyman should order him to stop.

He flung off his coat, hat, vest, and tie and settled into a steady jog. The moon began to set, and he knew that in two hours he would be free. Then a cramp caught him in the calf. With a roar of "God save me!" he tumbled on his back.

The cry saved him, for a witch cannot endure to hear the name of God. He saw a brief vision of scurrying forms, heard growling, hissing, and cursing in strange phrases, realized for a second that a hideous shape hung threateningly over him.

When he recovered, he found two portraits of the witch he danced with etched in fire on the handle of his jackknife, one as she appeared when he met her, and the other as she looked when his eyes were closing. Shortly after he got home, Tom became ill. When he regained his health he took to himself a wife, joined the church, forsook all entertainments, drank tea, and became a steady workman. He recovered his peace of mind, died a deacon, and was rewarded by having a cherub with a toothache sculptured on his gravestone.

CHAPTER 10

• • • • • • • • • • •

NELL HILTON'S GHOST

It is possible that many of the residents of the Jonesboro area in Maine have never heard of the ghost of Nell Hilton. A bit of folklore which comes from the northeastern Maine coastal region concerns this woman, whose ghost is said to appear on the anniversary of her death in years when America is or will be engaged in war.

Nell Hilton was a colonial girl who, in 1740, became tired of the coldness and strictness of life in Plymouth, and prevailed upon her father to move to the Passamaquoddy country so that they might enjoy a little more freedom of action. She proposed to have her own share of it in her own way, for her father, returning to his cabin in Jonesboro on a certain evening, found her in the embraces of a big Indian and submitting with smiles to his kisses. After killing and scalping this red man, Hilton learned that the girl had just engaged herself to him as his future wife. In disgust Hilton told her that if she was so fond of Indians she could go and live with them. She accepted his suggestion, moving out "bag and baggage."

At this time, it is said, the Americans would sell no powder to the natives, while the French in Canada would sell no rum. Because of this the savages had to travel constantly, bartering skins in the south for ammunition with which to get more skins, and selling skins in the north for strong waters in which to "pickle their own skins."

With her gift of language, Nell's services were in demand at the frontier as bargain-maker and interpreter, for she spoke French and Indian as well as English, and often taught school in Maine and New Brunswick. Nell Hilton never married, but she concentrated on getting power over the natives. In turn, the Indians regarded her as a queen and invited her to all their councils.

When the English drove the Acadians from Nova Scotia, she foretold the war that was to follow and advised the Indians to remain true to the French, who had exhibited more regard for their physical if not their moral life than had been shown by the English.

In 1775 Nell reappeared among her neighbors in Jonesboro to urge them to prepare for war, outlining the course of the Revolution from the Lexington skirmish right down to the Yorktown surrender. In 1777 she was captured by Tories and carried to St. John for trial as a Yankee spy. Although everyone who knew Nell testified to her many virtues and accomplishments, she was declared guilty and hanged. On the gallows she promised to be true to the American people and revisit them on March 1, her death-day anniversary, whenever they were to prepare for war. On her rock of prophesy at Hilton's Neck, she would speak to the people.

Tradition says that before her death she foretold the French and Indian trouble and the Revolution. After she died, we are told, her ghost, standing high on the rock, prophesied the war with England in 1812, with Mexico in 1846, the Civil War of 1861, the Spanish American War of 1898, and World War I. There seems, however, to be a dispute as to whether she foretold World War II.

PART FOUR

. . . .

True Tales

CHAPTER 1

. . . .

DEAD MAN'S LEDGE

Gull Head, located along the Maine coast, so I am told, is not too far from Dead Man's Ledge. I have never visited there. The ledge has borne that gruesome title ever since the discovery more than a century and a half ago of the body of a man tangled in the rockweed and kelp. Fishermen who found him noticed that he was swinging under water in grotesque fashion as the surges of the sea pulled him back and forth.

Shortly afterward the mariners found the wreckage of a schooner that had pounded to pieces the night before. Ever since that year many people who live in the vicinity of the headland have claimed that they could hear the man crying and shrieking just before a storm was coming up.

In spite of this superstition, generations later John Brown and his wife Bess moved into the cabin of a barkentine which had been wrecked near the ledge. Pulled up high on the shore above the reach of the tide, it was ideal for the couple. John Brown became a lobsterman and added to his earnings by taking odd jobs, clam digging, and farming near the headland. With the passing years he developed into an expert beach-comber, often being the first to find valuable wreckage as it washed up along the shore. In spite of his diversified life, Brown was a sturdy soul. Many of his friends jokingly called him a wrecker and mooncusser, but never in his life had he shown a false beacon or recovered from the sea and retained property which he knew belonged to others.

The joy of his old age was his teen-age foster daughter, Nell, a "precious bit of flotsam" who, as a baby, had been brought ashore from a shipwreck. A fourth resident of the area was Antonio, a quiet dark-faced Spaniard who was one of several survivors from the shipwreck of a bark from Málaga, Spain. Heavily laden with oranges and cigars, the Spanish craft had scattered her cargo up and down the coast. Antonio sometimes helped Brown in his work on the boats, and as the months went by became interested in eighteen-year-old Nell.

The following year, during a wintry storm, a yacht capsized near Gull Head. Only one survivor reached shore, twenty-one-year-old Edward Irving of Richmond, Virginia. When Irving saw Nell for the first time, he was attracted to the girl, who indeed was beautiful. Deciding to apply for a job as a fisherman so that he could stay in the area, Edward became a member of the crew of a local fishing schooner.

Although a sailor, Irving was a man of taste, breeding, and manners. Antonio saw with misgiving that Nell apparently had become interested in the newcomer with a depth of feeling she had never shown toward him. The Spaniard was discouraged when he realized that Irving had so much more to tell of the life in America outside the fishing village than he, a European, ever could. He began to take long walks, and as he hiked he started the habit of muttering to himself, his eyes flashing dangerously from time to time.

More and more Nell and Edward were oserved strolling along the shore. Stealthily, Antonio began shadowing them. His moodiness and silence increased, for as he shadowed the couple he was forming dangerous plans which could result in death in the ocean for Irving. Knowing of the latter's interest in sea shells, he proposed one summer evening that Irving should go with him out to Dead Man's Ledge where brilliant purple shells were found if enough effort was expended.

With a promise to return shortly, the two men sailed off together. Arriving at Dead Man's Ledge, they noticed that the rock was but three feet above the incoming tide. At high water the sea would be more than a fathom over the ledge.

The two men went ashore on the rock and began searching for the attractive purple shells. Knowing that the time was short, Irving worked so diligently hunting for the shells that he thought of nothing else. Preoccupied, he did not notice Antonio as he casually wandered back to the boat, nor did he observe the Spaniard's black scowl as he clambered in and cast off.

Suddenly, as Irving heard the sound of the sail being hauled into place, he realized what was occurring—Antonio was abandoning him on the rock. Uttering a weird laugh, the Spaniard threw down the helm, swung about, and sailed off on a freshening wind.

"Enough of your pranks," shouted Irving. "You have enjoyed your joke. Take me aboard. You know the tide is coming in fast."

In answer the Spaniard showed his teeth in a snarl. Shouting a curse at Irving, Antonio told him to die as a dog. Antonio let out the sail, and ten minutes later the craft disappeared around the headland.

Still unable to believe that Antonio was really leaving him to die, Irving waited for the craft to return. By the time twilight had given way to complete darkness, he was standing waist-deep in water on the ledge and realized that he had been abandoned to certain death. But what would cause Antonio to do such a thing? Could it be on account of his love for Nell? Of course it was. Why had he been so blind?

With the tide up to his chest, Irving noticed that the moon

was rising, and he concluded that its light was the last illumination he would ever look upon. The hopelessness of his situation was quite apparent, and he decided that in his last moments he would pray that his sins be forgiven. Then he thought of the girl who had smiled happiness into his heart so short a time before, and in desperation he shouted out her name, "Nell, Nell!" He called louder and louder, and then, despite his distress, he half-smiled at his folly. Of course he was miles beyond her hearing, and yet it seemed to relieve his feeling of desperation. The moon came up, and soon its glow illuminated the scene.

Suddenly, out on the sea he saw a long black object coming his way in a crosscurrent. Perhaps it was a shark, but as it floated without animation he concluded it could not be alive. As it swept even closer he recognized it as a spar. If only he could swim out and reach it, he might still save himself. One thing he knew—death was certain if he stayed on Dead Man's Ledge. He must chance his strength against wind and tide. Throwing off his shoes and jacket, he plunged into the waves, swimming slowly and surely toward his goal. After an exhausting struggle he reached the timber, straddled it, and used a strand of rope hanging from the spar to tie himself on. As the current carried him away from the ledge, Irving prayed even more earnestly than before.

How long he drifted he could not tell, but although it seemed like days, it was actually only hours. Dawn was breaking when in a period of half wakefulness, he seemed to hear shouting. Irving listened intently. Indeed, a faint cry did come to his ears, and he replied with a shout. The call was repeated from time to time, a little louder at each repetition, and each time he answered. At last, as he shifted his position on the spar, Edward sighted a boat sailing toward him. The first voice he heard was that of old John.

"Luff, there, Nell. Steady. Here he is. God's name, lad,

how came ye in this fix? Give a hand. Easy, now. There ye are. Where's Tony? Where's the boat? Nell, you see you couldn't have heard Mr. Edward call your name, but you were right in guessing he was in danger. Women are mostly— Well, I don't mind your kissing him, considering. Don't cry. He's only chilled up a bit. We'll have him before the fire in half an hour, and this old sail will cover him meantime. But what happened to the boat?"

The old man's rage and astonishment were boundless when he learned of Antonio's treachery. Two days later neighbors came to report that they had found a body on Dead Man's Ledge. It was that of Antonio, drowned in the sea.

CHAPTER 2

· · · · · · · · · ·

THE PRIVATEER *DASH*,
PRIDE OF PORTLAND

In my *Legends of the New England Coast,* which came out in 1957, I included a chapter on phantom ships of the area. Since that time I have had many letters asking for more details on one of the "phantom" craft included, the *Dash,* about which John Greenleaf Whittier wrote in his poem "The Dead Ship of Harpswell."

Indeed, one of the most interesting relics brought to light during the work of collecting Maine's exhibit for the 1893 World's Fair was a model of the craft. The *Dash,* begun in 1812, was a vessel that never found her superior in speed until the days of the clipper ships. Chased for months by the best ships in the British navy, she was never captured. Taking valuable prizes, she maintained her position upon the sea through the War of 1812, and only succumbed to the element upon which she had won her triumphs, going down at the height of a winter's gale.

The record of this craft, as her papers remain to show, was one which even fancy has not improved upon. The "Ariel" of Cooper was not the equal of this Maine craft.

Even in her inception, the *Dash* was unique. At that time

the later plan of drafting vessels was practically unknown, and the solid model was undreamed of. The prevailing practice was simply to lay a keel, set up at either end a stem and stern post, and fill in between the frames, shaping the hull "by the eye," as the work progressed.

Of course the results of this sort of building were not always satisfactory, the two sides of the vessel being seldom the same shape, so that a craft would frequently sail faster on one tack than she would on the other.

However, the builders of the *Dash* wanted a craft that could show the highest type of speed. They realized that in the service for which she was designed such a vessel must either be a flyer or a failure. Being experienced shipwrights as well as shipowners, they were able to call practical knowledge to their assistance in the solution of this problem; and the first ship's model that the State of Maine ever knew was the result. Of course it was unlike the solid models which came afterward. Upon a backboard, pieces of wood to represent halves of frames were nailed, thin layers of wood were tacked upon them, and thus the skeleton of one half of a vessel was made. By repeated trimmings and cuttings, the lines of the hull were perfected until what seemed to be the required shape for speed had been secured, after which the keel was laid.

The men who ventured upon construction of this craft were John and Seward Porter of Portland, and the vessel was built in their yard at Porter's Landing, their old home.

Only a few rotten piles of the wharf from which the *Dash* was launched now remain; the yard where so many fine vessels were built has long since been overrun by grass; but this model has been preserved carefully as an heirloom.

The model is especially interesting to marine architects of today because it is an unanswerable refutation of the claim, so often made, that the sharp floor lines of the modern yacht did not exist until the 1890s. Made in 1812, the model, except for its almost perpendicular sternpost, might easily be mistaken for a craft of the Burgess class, the bow being sharp, the run beginning amidships, and all the floor timbers at a sharp angle. All her lines are very suggestive of the world-renowned Boston clippers of the eighteen fifties.

The *Dash* was not, however, originally designed to be a privateer; she was merely a natural product of the times. For years both English and French vessels had been troubling the Americans, and when the embargo was ordered, no ordinary craft could venture to sea with any prospect of success. Therefore ships lay dismantled at the wharves or swung idly in harbors, warehouses went uncared for, and the merchant marine of the United States was literally paralyzed. Then it was that some venturesome men possessed themselves of fleet craft and, defying danger, made immense profits out of risky voyages, since West India products sold at exorbitant prices. So, when war was formally declared, the Porters built this vessel to run the gauntlet of English warships between Cuba and Portland, much as the blockade-runners operated during the Rebellion.

As E. C. Plummer wrote in 1894, the risk which these vessels ran at that time can be better appreciated when it is remembered that the United States was then practically without a navy. Only five of our craft could be rightly claimed as fighting ships, while England had more than eighty vessels regularly cruising in these waters. During the war Great Britain sometimes showed more than one hundred sail in the North Atlantic. But the superiority of American ships over those of foreign build, and the unequaled skill of American sailors, had even then been demonstrated; and Yankee confidence was fully equal to the emergency.

Completed in 1813, the *Dash* was rigged as a topsail schooner—a favorite style in those days. Her home port was

Portland, and there she was fitted for the sea. She first slipped down to Santo Domingo unobserved, disposed of a cargo at good prices, loaded with coffee, and was well on her way home, when she was sighted by a British man-of-war, which sent a cannon ball invitation for her to come about and await the pleasure of His Majesty's representative.

But Captain Kelleran, an officer well known in his day, was in command, and he would not entertain the idea of losing his handsome vessel on her maiden trip; so he simply piled on the canvas, pitched overboard enough of his cargo to let his little schooner take her racing form, and permitted the Englishman to fade slowly away in the distance, though the foremast was badly sprung and nearly taken out of the *Dash* by the strain.

She returned to Portland safely, having proved herself an excellent sailer. But her master had noticed that by altering her sail plan she could be made to give an even better account of herself. So the split foremast was removed, a heavier spar put in its place, and square sails added, making the *Dash* a hermaphrodite brig. A tremendous spread of light sails was given her, and then, like many of the later Gloucester fishermen, she was ready to tackle anything that came her way.

One of the disadvantages under which the *Dash* labored, like most American vessels of those days, was lack of sheathing, copper being very costly. Thus the unprotected bottom became foul very quickly, while the British cruisers, sheathed in metal, were always in racing trim. The Yankee captain avoided this handicap, in a measure, by giving his craft a coating of tallow and soap just before starting out on a voyage. Although this mixture soon wore away, it was good while it lasted, an added advantage being that both soap and tallow were cheap.

Having been thus prepared, the *Dash* started out once more. British war vessels began a chase of her almost at once, one of them no less than a seventy-four-gun ship. She sailed away from them as usual and landed her cargo in good order, but at the height of one of the races she had to sacrifice her two bow guns and part of her deckload to get into necessary flying trim. The fact that coffee was then selling at one dollar per pound still made the profits from this voyage highly satisfactory.

So far the mission of the *Dash* had been a peaceful one. All her captain asked was that she be left alone. But now came the days when the American sailor was standing up to the English on the high seas. The fighting fever was upon the people, and because of this a new captain was appointed to the *Dash*. A new feeling of confidence developed in New England privateering circles, and it was agreed that taking cargo was easier than purchasing it in foreign ports. The *Dash* was now fitted out as a first-class privateer with all the guns necessary.

The small broadside guns which she had been carrying for her own protection were removed, and two eighteen-pounders were taken instead. The "long Tom" or "thirty-two" which had been mounted amidships was retained.

A larger crew was needed and shipped, and the *Dash* started out, not exactly looking for trouble, but with the avowed purpose of doing less running in the future. The captain vowed that he would take charge of the first British merchantman sighted.

Unfortunately, she ran into a giant British seventy-four-gun man-of-war. The seventy-four was not the kind of game she was seeking, and the *Dash* fled under full sail, quickly dropping the man-of-war below the horizon. Shortly afterward she was approached by a cruiser only slightly larger than her own size, showed fight, won a victory, and carried a precious cargo to port.

Then came a spectacular record of prizes. Encountering

the armed ship *Lacedemonian,* she captured her, together with the American sloop which the British ship was carrying off in triumph. A little later the *Dash* was chased by a frigate and a schooner. She outsailed the frigate, drew the schooner away from the protection of the big ship, whipped her soundly, and went on her way rejoicing.

Her captain at this time was a young man whose merits President Lincoln subsequently recognized by making him inspector of customs at Portland. Captain William Cammett, a dyed-in-the-wool sailor, was a man who never saw the Union Jack but that he felt a desire to fight.

The *Dash* continued her successful career, taking cargoes out of the English vessels when she could find them, buying them in port when she could not, and capturing many prizes, until she had made herself a terror to the British merchant marine. She was the pride of Portland, but the object of a most emphatic hatred on the part of the British man-of-war's sailor, who could no more catch her than he could corner the will-o'-the-wisp.

Finally she was put under the command of Captain John Porter, a young brother of the owners, then but twenty-four years of age, but a youth who had already established a fine record on the quarter-deck. He made two captures within a week from the time he left port. The *Dash* retook the American privateer *Armistice,* which had just fallen a prey to the English frigate *Pactolus,* and a few days later added two brigs and a sloop to the list. When Captain Porter came back to port to refit, having been absent less than three months, he had already sent home six prizes to prove that the time had not been wasted.

Under Porter's command, the *Dash* reached the zenith of her glory. She could show a record unsurpassed by any other American privateer. She had never known a reverse, had never attacked a vessel in vain, had never been injured by an enemy shot, and it was claimed that her equal in speed did not exist. Thus it was that young men came to compete for the privilege of signing on as members of her crew.

The day had arrived when it was considered a high honor to be pointed out as belonging to the *Dash,* for it was the equivalent of saying that here was a man or youth who had made the grade. Men from families in Portland and surrounding towns made up her force, and every family sending a representative aboard the *Dash* was proud of the honor.

Her history was a glorious one when she started on that last and fatal cruise. It was the middle of January 1815. Unconscious of the fact that a treaty of peace between the United States and Great Britain had already been signed, the crew of the *Dash* were impatient to be away after more glory and more prize money. The light canvas was crowded upon the tall, tapering masts, and, ready for sea, the rakish craft was dashing up and down the harbor waiting for the coming of the captain, who alone of the ship's company was not on board.

Meanwhile their commander was bidding farewell to his young wife. Married but a few months, the young couple seemed to know by instinct that they should not part and that this would be their last meeting. The signal gun had sounded for him, but still Captain Porter did not heed its summons. He lingered until a second gun told him that he must obey the call, and then he hurried away to the landing.

What little more is known of the *Dash* is told by the crew of the *Champlain,* a new privateer which had waited in the harbor to try her speed against that of the Portland champion on an outward cruise.

Leaving the harbor together, they took a southerly course. The *Dash* drew away to the front, and at the close of the next day was far in the lead. Then a gale came on, and the last seen of the *Dash* she was shooting away into the driving clouds of snow which soon hid her from sight. As he feared Georges shoals, the master of the *Champlain* altered his course and came out of the gale in safety, but nothing more was ever heard of the *Dash*.

Probably Captain Porter, with the crude instruments of those days, failed to estimate his speed correctly and was on the shoals before he suspected his danger. All who have seen the miles of breakers hurrying over these "rapids of the sea" can understand why sailors fear them so, and possibly the *Dash* foundered there.

For months, even years, those whose loved ones had gone out aboard the *Dash* refused to believe them lost. Year followed year, however, with never a word of hope. The steps of those who for so many long months had climbed to the high observatory on Munjoy Hill to ask if any news had come grew less frequent upon the stair. The thought that some time at least one of the crew would come back to tell the vessel's fate was gradually forgotten and mothers came to know their sons were dead. Never a piece of wreckage reached the shore. No floating spar or splintered boat ever appeared to offer its mute testimony. The vessel had as completely disappeared as if she had been one of her own cannon balls dropped into the sea, and only the records of her successful voyages remain.

Bror Tamm of Quincy, Massachusetts, well-known naval architect, made a complete study of all the known facts concerning the *Dash*.

"All indications are that she capsized. Hell-bent for speed, she had a big crew and probably went right over on her beam ends."

CHAPTER 3

. . . .

IS IT LOST FOREVER?

In the year 1866 a Boston resident named Henry Haggman, vacationing in Maine, discovered a strange character living the life of a hermit on Isle au Haut in Penobscot Bay.

The ferry from Rockland had landed Henry on the island, where he soon established himself at a boardinghouse not too far from the island pier. Early the next morning he started out for a day of pleasure with his gun, compass, box of matches, fishing rod, and sketchbook. Several hours later Haggman found himself on a rocky, hilly location where there were tall trees and treacherous ledges. Becoming confused with the terrain, he eventually admitted to himself that he was lost in an island forest. Henry sat down on a boulder and began to plan how to extricate himself from his predicament. He figured correctly that as he was on an island, if he started hiking toward the sun, taking a check with his compass every so often, eventually he would reach the ocean. Then he could follow the coastline and sooner or later he should come across some sort of settlement and get back to the place where he was staying on the island.

Although it was afternoon, he was not very tired, nor was he hungry. Nevertheless, the fact that he was lost made him ponder the question of how a man could live without available food. His gun and matches reassured him, but of course he wanted to get out of the woods by dark.

Gradually as he walked along he began to notice a sound which reminded him of the distant rumbling of a train passing over a bridge, but he realized there were no trains on the island. Walking in the direction of the constant roar, he soon discovered a waterfall cascading down over the rocks, after which it formed little eddies in a pool below.

When he looked down into the pool, he could see many colors at the bottom of the clear water and decided that here indeed was a delightful location. Then the clouds overhead separated, the sun came out, and he was in brilliant light. He now realized that he had a perfect chance to use his sketching pencil.

First he drew the outline, then the rocks, and soon was sketching the waterfall, using quick, decisive strokes. He added the pool, the ferns growing by the edge of the pool, and the deep water. Next he began outlining the trees standing in the background. He included each new subject that attracted his attention. Suddenly he was amazed by an unexpected object which he had begun to sketch without realizing what he was drawing.

Afraid at first that it was merely his imagination, Henry continued to sketch. Nevertheless, as he gradually realized, he was outlining the shape of a man standing near the massive trunk of an evergreen tree just above the falls. Henry concluded that if the figure was a real man, then indeed he was a veritable giant. His hair and beard were white as snow, with the beard hanging down almost to his waist.

"Hello!" shouted Henry. "Please, would you stand perfectly still for a minute or two? I want you in this picture I'm sketching."

The giant did not reply but did remain absolutely still.

For the next few minutes the artist's pencil was extremely active as the huge creature's figure took form in the drawing. As the pencil raced across the sketch pad, Henry's thoughts were of his strange subject. The giant stood erect, his posture giving prominence to his broad shoulders and husky build. Without question, Haggman thought, the man might have stood for a portrait of the famous Roman general Belisarius, or even Moses of Biblical fame.

A few minutes later Henry shouted out his thanks. "You may move as much as you please now," he cried.

To his amazement the figure answered in a loud, clear voice, "Away, intruder!"

In desperation Henry made the sign of a certain secret organization which is known all over the world. When Henry did this, the giant began to wave his arms wildly and cried out, "Who are you? Why do you invade my solitude?"

Henry answered, "I am a Bostonian spending a vacation on the island. I am lost in these woods. You just returned the sign of brotherhood. Why then do you order me away?"

"Young man," answered the giant, his voice gradually softening, "there is something about you which makes me think that you speak the truth, although I long ago lost all faith in mankind. Stay where you are; I will come to you."

The giant disappeared from the side of the ledge, and the silence which followed caused Henry to feel uneasy. He picked up his gun, made sure it was loaded and capped, and then stood it up in a position near at hand.

A few minutes later the hermit appeared, holding in his right hand a long, heavy rifle. Henry was just a little frightened, as he admitted later. He said to himself, "This is a madman, undoubtedly escaped from some lunatic asylum."

As the giant approached him, Henry repeated his statement. "I am an artist, and I came to the island for a few days' vacation. You gave me the sign of the brotherhood, and so why do you doubt me?"

"Well," came the reply, "since I turned my back on the world, I have trusted no one. In spite of this, if you give me the sacred word of the brotherhood, I will do what I can. Because the sun will soon set and it is too far to go back to the village, I'll protect you tonight and guide you to a safe place in the morning. Follow me."

Half an hour later the giant had led Henry to the top of another ledge. Then they approached a log cabin which proved to be half below and half above the ground, completely surrounded by bushes so that a hunter or surveying party might pass it without seeing the cabin at all.

Entering, Henry noticed that the cabin contained two rooms, each about twenty feet square. One was a living room, and the other a storeroom. There was a remarkably good assortment of carpenter's implements, firearms, and fishing tools hung against the wall, while the furniture in the log cabin consisted of a table, lounge chair, hammock, and a cot. There were no books or writing materials of any kind.

"Come," growled the giant. "You are my guest for the night."

Walking through the storeroom, the two men passed venison, lamb, fowl, and fish hung on pegs. There were eggs, a pan of milk, a pile of potatoes, a bushel of nuts, and in one corner a sack of flour.

Opening a small but strong door in the rear, the giant led Henry up several steps to an open space, an outdoor enclosure of triangular shape, containing about one-half acre of land. The entire area was surrounded by a small palisade made of the stumps of trees that the giant obviously had cut down. On the outside was a dense thicket of brambles and tall bushes completely covering the enclosure, so that any person passing that way would not have even imagined its existence.

"How long have you lived here?" asked Henry.

"I am sorry, but I will not tell you," replied the white-bearded hermit. "Why don't you let me see the picture you made of me?"

Henry handed him the sketch.

"Do I look like that?" asked the giant.

"Well, of course I am not really an artist and I would have to consider your question in the view of accuracy, but my opinion is that I have drawn a good likeness."

Lost in reflection for several minutes, the hermit finally spoke. "I believe you are right. The cascade, the pools, and the trees are all perfect, and so it stands to reason you have pictured me as I am."

Then Henry ventured to ask the old man a question. "Do you like this sort of life?"

The hermit gave a quick reply. "No one lies to me here, defrauds me, slanders me, or deceives me."

Henry then reminded the giant that it was impossible to live as he did without some connection with the world, for the giant's clothing, objects on his table, and many standard provisions in his storeroom indicated association with the outside world.

"It is true that I get an occasional sack of flour and the like, but I avoid all contact with humanity except four times a year. I make my appearances as brief as possible and never see the same parties twice in a row. Here I am like Robinson Crusoe. My goats, sheep, and fowl do not lie to me. Come now, we have talked long enough. You will sleep on the cot and I will sleep in the hammock. Unload your gun before retiring. I trust no one."

Henry unloaded his gun and retired to the cot. Soon he was sleeping soundly and did not awaken until sunrise. Getting up, he went down to the brook to wash with the hermit. In the stream he saw several trout and wondered if he could catch any for breakfast.

"May I fish for our breakfast?" inquired Henry.

"Yes," replied his host, "but you must not catch my largest and favorite trout. I call him Nebuchadnezzar."

Twenty minutes later Henry felt a mighty pull on his line. The hermit ran across at once and stood beside him.

"Cut the line! Cut the line!" cried the hermit.

But Henry brought the trout to the surface and before throwing the huge fish back, he estimated that Nebuchadnezzar weighed about eight pounds.

Ten minutes more fishing resulted in Henry's catching two moderate-sized trout, and an hour later they finished eating a fine breakfast. The hermit then pushed away from the table and told Henry that he must leave by three o'clock that afternoon.

When three o'clock arrived, the giant took Henry down to a fairly well-identified trail where they said goodby.

"You will not forget to keep our secret," said the giant.

Henry promised that he would keep his word, but he made a final effort to have the giant come back to civilization.

"No, I will not ever return to your world, regardless of the fact that I have never injured or wronged any human. My style of life now is quite different, but it is you who have a problem. I am wondering how you will explain your long overnight absence to your landlord in the village."

Henry thought for a few moments, and then said, "I will tell them I was lost and slept in the woods all night. Getting back to my thoughts of your existence here, I hope that someday I can find out more about why you have chosen this island abode."

The giant sat down on a nearby rock. "I am sixty-nine years old now," he began, "and I would say that probably I will not live more than fifteen years. Perhaps if you could come back about 1880 I might not mind what you reveal to the world."

The two men shook hands and parted company. Henry followed the trail down to what had evidently been a road which descended to the village.

When he returned to the cottage where he was staying, his newly-made friends accepted his explanations without comment, and he left for the mainland a few days later. After a week spent in Rockland, Maine, Henry went to Boston.

For the next few years Henry was active in the service of a Boston insurance firm. Each summer he thought that he would like to go back to Isle au Haut and see the hermit, but he did not make the effort. It was not until 1879, following a severe bout with pneumonia, that Henry realized he needed another good Maine vacation.

His doctor suggested that he should visit the Penobscot Bay area again but definitely warned him that he could explore that section of Maine only if he did not exert himself. Two weeks later Henry was aboard the ferry out of Rockland, Maine. On his way to Isle au Haut he passed Saddleback Ledge and noticed the new lighthouse which had been built on the rock there.

As the ferry passed through the Isle au Haut Thoroughfare, his thoughts turned to the hermit and he began to wonder if the giant would still be alive. On landing, he quickly established himself at a lodginghouse and made plans for a long hike the next morning.

At dawn he arose and ate a good breakfast. Two hours later he was atop a high peak from which he surveyed the area. Choosing a rocky ridge which apparently led to the sea, he penetrated the region where he believed he had first encountered the hermit. After quite a little effort he found the stream where he had caught and freed Nebuchadnezzar years before. He then laboriously made his way up what he recognized as a long-forgotten trail. With quickening step he came upon the triangular area around what he hoped was the cabin. The underbrush and brambles suggested that no one had been near here for quite a few years.

Making his way toward the place where he remembered the log cabin was located, he walked by it three times before he discovered the hermit's abode. The doorway was heavily covered with weeds and bushes of all descriptions. Indeed it was an almost impossible place to discover.

Reaching the door, Henry attempted to push it open but had no success. Walking around the house several times, he found all windows heavily boarded up, but did discover a small aperture which had been secured by a heavy timber. If he was to get into the house, he would have to smash the wooden obstruction.

He pondered the situation. Recalling that some distance back he had passed the trunk of a fallen tree, Henry retraced his steps. Although he could lift the trunk, he was not able to carry it in his weakened condition, and so he took off his coat and secured the garment around the end of the trunk. Henry put his shoulders under the coat-covered tree and started dragging it toward his objective.

Half an hour later he reached the cabin, although he was terribly exhausted. He realized that his body was drained of all strength and that he must rest to prevent a relapse. Indeed it was vital that he get into the cabin. Slinging a rope around a beam which jutted out from the eaves, he hoisted the stump into the air until the heavier end faced the aperture. Then he started it swinging as a pendulum back and forth, back and forth, crashing it into the timber time and again. Finally the timber splintered enough for the log to break it in. Smashing and smashing with renewed effort, he opened an aperture large enough for him to enter. After resting a few minutes, he then squeezed himself through the window frame.

Henry fumbled around in the semidarkness until he found a candle which he lighted. By this illumination he was able to walk to the front door, where he removed three heavy bars securing the entrance.

Walking around the cabin, Henry lifted the solid wooden barriers from each window one by one and was grateful for the sunlight which filtered in. Soon there was enough light to permit him to look around and identify objects in the house. He recognized the cot which the hermit had allowed him to use that fateful night thirteen years before. On a table by the cot he noticed a small wooden box which he had never seen before.

Haggman picked up the box, and to his surprise, he discovered his own name written in pencil on the box with the words, "To be opened by Henry Haggman only."

Henry sat down and pried up the cover, after which he emptied the contents, one by one, on the table. A bundle done up in vellum was just inside the cover, and he examined it carefully. There was a personal message tied by string on the outside of the vellum-wrapped package. He read it aloud:

To Henry Haggman,

It is my hope that you will return some day to this cabin and find this message. It is now 1876, many years since your visit. My last days are approaching. I am sealing up this cabin. With your ingenuity I trust that you will find a way to break in, for I know how curious you were.

I have not decided how to end my life, but I will do so within a week. You may do anything you wish with the material you find inside the vellum. It will explain much in which you may show interest. One thing, however, you must carry out. I warn you not to stay in the cabin or on the island more than forty-eight hours. Unless I have miscalculated, this cabin should be entirely destroyed within a few days of your leaving it.

You will not be blamed for what will take place. All you have to do is to throw open the long trap door in the roof. Do not open anything else in this box until you arrive at your home.

Henry carried out the hermit's orders carefully. Within four hours he had opened the asbestos-covered trap door, secured the cabin windows and the front door, and then returned along the trail which led down to the Isle au Haut village. Before sunset he had gathered together his belongings and was on his way to the mainland. From Rockland he took a stagecoach to Portland and arrived in Boston four days later.

In his home on Beacon Hill he had one room to which he could go on special occasions and lock himself in. That following Sunday night he carried the package wrapped in vellum to this private room and there carefully cut the leather thongs.

There were five objects inside the package. The first thing that attracted Henry's attention was a cabinet photograph of a beautiful young lady. Next he found a diary for the year 1852. The three other objects were sealed envelopes, one of which was addressed to Henry, another was marked "My family," and the third proved to be a collection of clippings of the years 1851 and 1852.

After spending some time examining the photograph of the girl, Henry opened the letter addressed to himself.

"Dear Henry Haggman," the letter read, "As I indicated to you earlier, I have lost faith in civilization and have taken this method of staying away from almost all of humanity. If you have followed my instructions, you are now back on the mainland.

"In the year 1851 I met a beautiful girl during the summer

at Newport. In the fall, as we were both residents of Boston, I called at her house on several occasions and soon became more than interested in combining her future with mine. She agreed that we would be married in the spring. The wedding took place in June.

"As my means were then substantial, I purchased a fine residence on West Street near the Common, and we were very happy. I had to travel extensively in those days between Boston and New York, where I was establishing a brokerage firm.

"One wintry night I bade my wife farewell and took a hansom cab to the railroad depot. Unfortunately a terrible snowstorm developed and the train could not leave the station. I returned to my West Street home. Opening the door with my latch key, I was quite mystified by the signs of snow-tracked footprints in the vestibule, and outside my living room I could hear a commotion. My wife's voice I plainly heard, together with that of a man.

"Sickened by my discovery, I had no desire but to leave at once. I walked out of the house through the snow storm. At a hotel in Scollay Square I signed the register as Leonard Partridge. The next morning, a Tuesday, I went down to the first of the two banks in which I kept my funds. Withdrawing all of my belongings from the safe deposit vault, I then consulted with the vice president of the bank who agreed to carry out my plans to the letter. The next day, with $50,000 of my money changed into gold pieces, I hired a cab and was soon out of town.

"Two hours later I was in Worcester where I dismissed the cab. I took another conveyance from Worcester to Springfield to cover my tracks, and then by carriage I arrived at Lee, Massachusetts. At Lee I visited a store where I purchased an old iron Wells-Fargo chest. I hired another horse and carriage and was soon out of town with the gold and the chest. Some hours later I arrived in Bolton. Near the junction of the road on which I traveled I found a relatively deserted house and barn. Although it appeared to have been in recent use, there was no sign of life on the property. I discovered a large well or cistern which suited my purpose, and I lowered the iron chest into the water. I left the area and returned to Lee. Two days later in Boston I arranged for my second banker to place $20,000 from my other account in a bank in the Penobscot Bay area, and eventually built my cabin on the island.

"So thus my simple story comes to an end. As you seem to have an inquisitive mind, if you are inclined to try to find the gold which is at the bottom of the cistern, I hereby give you permission to go ahead and claim it.

"Regarding my wife, my bank associate followed her career. She died after a few years, a victim of consumption."

Henry never revealed what the other documents stated, nor did he ever learn how the giant's life ended. However, he always believed that he was responsible for the forest fire which roared across a section of the Isle au Haut a few days after his departure.

Actually, as Henry later learned from the giant's effects, the recluse had devised a very careful scheme of burning down his log cabin. High in a tree the hermit had secured a powerful lens so that the sun, catching the lens during the summer, would direct the light against an asbestos hatch cover in the roof, which when open would allow the sunbeams to pass through the hole and focus on a point fourteen feet inside. Thus if the sun were shining it would start a conflagration in a pile of dried leaves and cotton on the floor there. If the asbestos hatch cover remained closed, the lens could not focus and set fire to the leaves inside.

Although Henry never went back to the scene of the fire to check on the lens in the tree and what really consumed the log cabin, he read enough in the local papers to realize that undoubtedly it was his act of leaving the hatch cover off which really caused the fire.

On several occasions Henry visited the town of Bolton. He never did record all of his activities in the area, but when he died his heirs found enough evidence to assemble some of the amazing pieces in the puzzle of what did take place in Bolton.

In the beginning, when the giant had reached Bolton to hide his treasure chest, he found a cisternlike well on a relatively deserted estate as is mentioned above. It was ideal for the hiding of the iron chest containing the gold. The giant completed a careful map of the area on which he identified Spindle Hill, Mattaquatic Hill, and Vaughn Hill. Today Spindle Hill can still be identified on a map which also includes State Highway 117 and Route 85.

Years later, at the time Henry was tracing down the identifications on the giant's map of the Bolton, Massachusetts, region, he soon reached the general location where the hermit stated that he had lowered the chest into the well. It was only by accident that he found the cistern in one corner of the property. Having decided not to tell anyone that he was in the area, he soon discovered that the farm was vacant and that he had a very good chance to explore the cistern for several hours every day.

By careful planning and studying, Henry was able to keep at his task. To get down into the well he purchased a long wooden ladder which he placed in the cistern. The next day he descended twelve feet into the cistern until he reached the surface of the water, where he employed an impromptu boat hook to probe the bottom of the cistern. One day when the sun was brilliant in intensity, a beam pierced the semidarkness of the cistern and Henry noticed a four-inch eyebolt in the cistern wall. The bolt had rusted through. Henry recalled in the giant's notes the mention of a bolt in the cistern wall through which the hermit had run a length of chain.

Time and again Henry descended the ladder and probed with the hook. Finally his efforts paid off, and he came in contact with a chain which he pulled to the surface.

Henry became excited when he discovered that he was unable to release the end of the chain from the bottom of the well.

Could it still be fastened to the treasure chest? He strained and pulled but made no progress. By noon he was very tired, and so he decided to secure the chain to an under-water rung of the ladder. He then returned home.

On his next trip he divided his time into alternate periods of work and rest. Finally the chain slackened just a little, and he felt it give several inches. Unfortunately, when he pulled again the chain appeared as tight as ever. Evidently the chest, if chest it was, had caught on an underwater encumbrance.

Straining his utmost, Henry failed to make further progress and again stopped his efforts.

A week intervened, during which time he obtained a twenty-foot-long piece of two-by-four timber. Returning to the cistern, he probed down into the well with the timber until he could outline the shape of the underwater object. He soon realized that it was probably a heavy metal box and might easily be a typical Wells-Fargo money chest. There was, however, an evident jutting-out of the well wall which was preventing his raising the chest to the surface.

Henry figured that if he moved the position of the ladder to a point opposite the metal chest, the new angle would allow him to pull the object across and up to the surface. By this time, of course, he was again getting tired, and so he stopped for the day.

It was ten o'clock the next morning when Henry determinedly descended the ladder. Within half an hour he had dislodged the chest from under the ledge. He strained and pulled for almost an hour. Then the chain went slack for the second time within a few days.

Eagerly Henry tightened his grip on the chain. The chest rose slowly from the bottom of the well. Less than a minute later Henry watched an iron box break the surface of the water, and was elated. Unfortunately, as he soon became aware, it was much easier to pull the chest up to the surface than it was to lift the heavy box out of the water. Tugging and pulling again, he began to realize that he was not making any progress. In desperation he tried to get one corner of the chest to rest on a rung of the ladder, but failed completely.

Frantic with frustration, he strained and strained to the limit of his power. The result was absolute failure.

Eventually, wet with perspiration, he gave up. Utterly crushed in defeat, he allowed the treasure chest to sink down into the depths again, out of sight, and watched the chain drop down after it. So exhausted that he could barely climb the ladder and get out of the cistern, Henry waited a few minutes and then pulled the ladder from the well and carried it into the barn. There he covered it with hay, after which he collapsed in the hay and lost consciousness.

More than an hour passed before he recovered his senses enough to stand up on his feet and start for home. He was completely worn out. Hours later when he reached his Beacon Street residence in Boston, he was so exhausted that he decided to call the doctor. After the examination, the physician told Henry in no uncertain terms that he would not be responsible for Henry's life unless Haggman followed doctor's orders to the letter for the next few months.

"Stay in bed for at least a week," the doctor admonished him, "and then I'll call again. Remember, Henry, that you are no longer a boy of eighteen."

Henry realized reluctantly that the doctor's words of wisdom should be followed, and dismissed from his mind all thoughts of the fabulous treasure chest in the cistern at Bolton.

Henry Haggman did recover to live several more years, but he never returned to Bolton. When he died in 1882, his relatives studied all papers they could find pertaining to the hermit, Isle au Haut, and Henry's visit to Bolton. Henry had written excellent notes of all the experiences he had gone through in connection with the treasure chest and the hermit, but no member of his immediate family ever showed enough real interest to take an active part in the recovery of the Wells-Fargo chest.

Those who examined the papers were particularly impressed by two of Haggman's sketches which were found with the written material. One was of Henry's first encounter with the giant on the island, and the other was of Henry himself struggling with the treasure chest in the cistern.

In 1957 I drove by the residence and barn where, presumably, the cistern still held the chest. In 1967, when I made my last visit to the Bolton area to check on several points in the story, I found that the residence and the farm building where both the hermit and Henry had been active had vanished, and in their place was the junction of a highway.

Mrs. Henry Whitcomb, editor of the *History of Bolton,* who is well acquainted with the area in question, told me that it was not the first time the residence near the well had been moved. She explained that in 1793 the building was taken to the spot where both the hermit and Henry had found it, but around 1960 plans were made for it to be moved again.

Circumferential Highway 495 necessitated the removal of both house and barn, and the action took place in 1963. The ancient edifice is now in a new location on Route 85.

Mrs. Whitcomb took me over to the site of the house, barn, and well in November 1967, and we walked around the old estate. She explained that there were two wells, one under the residence itself and the other near the barn. The well near the barn, she told me, was the only one of the two which would qualify as the scene where the hermit submerged his gold.

Although Highway Engineer Joseph R. Shields believes that it is possible the well or cistern could be quite a distance underground now because of the ramps leading up to the highway, Mrs. Whitcomb does not agree in full. Finding the well, she believes, may not be the difficult task that it seems, as the top of the well may be relatively near the present level of the surrounding ground.

CHAPTER 4

• • • • • • • • • •

CAPE ELIZABETH

I have often visited Cape Elizabeth in Maine to enjoy for myself the scene which a nationally famous artist, the late Edward Hopper, painted of the lighthouse there. That outstanding picture graces the jacket of my *Famous Lighthouses of America* volume.*

Twin lights were built at Cape Elizabeth in the year 1827 to take the place of a monument erected years earlier as an aid to navigation, but only the lower light now sends its gleam across the waves.

In the long history of the Cape many thrilling episodes have occurred. I include three in this chapter. One took place in 1885 and the others in 1947.

On January 28, 1885, the wife of Keeper Marcus A. Hanna sighted a schooner's masts down near the rocks.

The weather had been fair but cold the day before, with a light wind blowing in from the northeast. Toward dusk the breeze freshened, and by midnight a severe storm swept in from the sea. Keeper Hanna, who had been sick with a bad cold, was doing his best to conquer his miserable feelings and make sure that the giant fog signal blast was operating at the height of its efficiency.

* Published in 1955, it is now out of print.

But his was a hopeless task. The wind increased, the snow fell in unprecedented heaviness, and the waves, although the tide was low, were soon smashing against the ledges around the headland. By three in the morning Keeper Hanna realized that no ship at sea could possibly hear the steam whistle, although he kept sounding the blasts every minute of the night.

He felt very ill and tried to ward off an intense desire to sleep. Finally, at six in the morning, Assistant Keeper Hiram Staples reported at the fog signal house for Hanna's relief. By this time, according to Hanna, "one of the coldest and most violent storms of snow, wind, and vapor was raging that I have ever witnessed."

When he started back to his home from the fog station, Hanna encountered great drifts three to five feet high and in his weakened condition had to crawl through the deeper snowdrifts to reach his home. Hanna's wife was waiting up for him, and after telling him that he should have known better than to go out on such a night, put Hanna to bed, announcing that she would attend to putting out the lamp in the lighthouse at the proper time. Keeper Hanna, exhausted from his cold and his struggle through the deep snowdrifts, soon fell asleep.

Mrs. Hanna, as many other faithful wives have done in their unsung careers at lonely lighthouse stations, extinguished the lamp in the tower at twelve minutes past seven, near sunrise. On her return from the lighthouse she went out of doors on the lee side of the building where there is a commanding view of the open sea. At twenty minutes before nine she suddenly saw, through the snow and vapor, the masts of a vessel loom up a quarter mile away. Mrs. Hanna rushed to her husband with the exciting but disheartening news.

"There is a vessel ashore near the fog signal!"

Hastily leaving his bed without a thought for himself, Keeper Marcus Hanna dressed at once and rushed out of the house. He floundered through the snowdrifts and soon reached the fog signal station, which was about two hundred yards from the wreck. Calling to Staples, Hanna found to his surprise that his assistant had not seen the wreck.

The unfortunate vessel was the schooner *Australia*, which had sailed from Boothbay Harbor, Maine, at five o'clock the evening before bound for Boston. Captain J. W. Lewis had a crew of two men, Irving Pierce and William Kellar, both seamen. When the storm hit them off Halfway Rock Light just before midnight, Captain Lewis had chosen to run for Portland, but later accepted the advice of Pierce to stand off instead. Shortly afterward the mainsail blew to pieces, and it was agreed to jog off and on under reefed foresail until morning. Because the temperature was down to four above zero, the *Australia* iced over so heavily that the crew was forced to throw over the deckload to keep the vessel afloat. They saw Cape Elizabeth Light at eight o'clock, and soon after the *Australia* grounded on the ledge below the beacon. A giant wave caught Captain Lewis and threw him down with great force, and before he could get up, the next wave hit, washing him over the side where he drowned. Just as the others were about to give up hope, they saw Keeper Hanna approaching with his assistant, who was sent at once for additional help.

Hanna reached the ice-covered rocks and attempted to throw a line aboard the schooner. Time after time he hauled back the icy cord and finally gave up. His wife had aroused neighbors and help was on the way. Suddenly a gigantic wave struck the schooner and lifted her bodily from the ledge across to the rocks where the fog signal station was located.

Keeper Hanna now threw his line and was overjoyed to

watch it land aboard the schooner. The men, however, could not free themselves from the shrouds to which they were frozen, and the line slid off into the sea. Keeper Hanna waded waist-deep into the sea, and by this time Pierce was able to break away from the icy coating which enveloped him. Hanna threw the line again and Pierce tied it around his waist.

Hanna realized that it would be almost impossible to pull the man in unaided, and cried desperately at the top of his voice for help. No one came, so he decided that he could wait no longer. Pierce signaled that he was ready, and went over the side into the sea. The lighthouse keeper hauled away. Wave after wave battered the frozen man as he was pulled to land. When he hit shore, Hanna was forced to pull him over the rocky ledge. Later Hanna said he never knew where he obtained the energy to pull and push the "helpless, frozen lump of humanity to a place out of reach of the surf." Irving Pierce was totally blind from exposure to the cold, and his jaws were frozen together. His whole appearance was ghastly. "The expression of his face," said Lighthouse Keeper Hanna later, "I shall not soon forget."

But there was still another shipwrecked mariner aboard the schooner, which was now going to pieces rapidly. Leaving Pierce for the moment, Keeper Hanna stumbled down to the shore again. Kellar had broken free of the shrouds, so Hanna adjusted the line and made his throw. Floating wreckage fouled the line, and he tried again and again. Finally it reached Kellar, who wound it around his icy body and signaled at once for the pull ashore. Although Hanna knew in his heart that he would not have strength enough to pull Kellar out of the ocean, he answered that he was ready and told Kellar to jump into the sea. The lighthouse keeper made a silent prayer that help would come in time, as his strength was failing fast.

As he began the torturous pull ashore, Keeper Hanna was greeted by shouts, and Assistant Staples together with two neighbors ran down the bank to help him. They had arrived just in time as if in answer to Keeper Hanna's prayer for aid. The four men soon had the helpless sailor out of the surf. Lifting the two mariners, they carried them through the deep drifts to the fog signal station. The frozen clothing of the two victims was cut off their bodies, and cold water rubbed on their limbs. Forcing open their jaws, the others poured stimulants down the throats of the shipwrecked victims. Dry flannels were put on the men, and they gradually regained their senses. The sailors were then given hot food and drink, and were soon able to tell their story. When they mentioned how their captain had been swept overboard, Hanna learned for the first time of the third man, Captain J. W. Lewis, who had been aboard the schooner. The captain's body later washed up on the shore near the scene of the disaster.

The snowstorm had been so severe that it was impossible to move the men from the fog signal station until the next day, when they were placed on a bobsled and taken to Hanna's residence. Two days later, as soon as roads were broken through from Portland, the survivors were taken to the city.

The second rescue in the vicinity occurred on March 3, 947, when the coal collier *Oakey L. Alexander* lost her bow ight miles out to sea in a terrible gale still remembered as the *"Oakey Alexander* storm." Strangely enough, another master also named Lewis was captain of the collier. After losing 135 feet of the vessel's bow, Captain Raymond Lewis called his crew together and found that every man was alive and well. In a voice of confidence he announced to the frightened men that he was bringing the stern of the collier in on the rocky ledges not too far from the gleam of a lighthouse which he recognized as Cape Elizabeth. He ordered the men back to their stations, and with skill and determination drove the broken collier through the surging billows until with a grinding crunch she struck the iron ledges of McKenny's Point. Gigantic waves smashed against the stern, shooting seventy feet into the air.

Over at Cape Elizabeth Coast Guard Station, Officer-in-charge Earle B. Drinkwater ordered the rescue gear made ready, and soon assembled his Lyle gun on the headland across from the wreck. The first projectile shot over the flying bridge, and the seamen on the *Alexander* made the line fast.

The tail block and the whip were sent out, and then the breeches buoy was attached to the whip's endless line.* Shortly after eight that morning the first survivor was landed by the breeches buoy, and within an hour all survivors were safely ashore.

Indeed it had been a double miracle, the first being that when the great craft had broken in two, no one had been on the bow, which disappeared at once beneath the waves. The second miracle was that Captain Lewis accomplished the unbelievable feat of bringing his crippled ship ashore, while the subsequent coast guard rescue allowed all on board to live.

Earlier that day the Canadian freighter *Novadoc,* twenty-two miles east of Cape Elizabeth, had radioed a distress signal that her condition was very serious. She was shipping water through a broken hatch, and was then "running before the wind."

No one will ever know just what happened after that, but around seven o'clock that night Lighthouse Keeper Clifton

---

* A tail block has an attached rope which can be used to tie the block onto a support. The whip is an endless line run through the block and used to haul the hawser on which the breeches buoy is slung. The breeches buoy is actually an enclosed canvas seat with openings for the legs.

Morang and his wife observed rocket after rocket shooting into the sky far out at sea from Cape Elizabeth.*

"There were fifteen or twenty rockets in all," reminisced Mrs. Morang later at Cape Elizabeth. "One right after the other at first, and then they came in slower intervals. Finally the last one shot up into the sky fifteen minutes after its predecessor. We notified the Coast Guard Base, and the *Cowslip* went out, but when she reached the vicinity, there was nothing in sight, not even wreckage. It must have been the *Novadoc*, just before she went down, for there was no other vessel in the vicinity."

The solution of where the *Novadoc* went down may be revealed some day. A prominent scuba diver informed me not too long ago that he has located what probably is the *Novadoc*, but until he has obtained certain items on board, his secret as to where the craft went down will remain his own.

---

* Indeed, it is an awesome feeling to witness this, as I did in the middle of the Atlantic at the height of World War II. We were members of the Eighth Bomber Command, gathered on the deck of the transport *Coamo*. Formerly active between New York and the West Indies, the *Coamo* left Liverpool after we disembarked and then vanished completely. I often think of that night when those of us aboard the *Coamo* watched the distress signals from an unknown craft probably going down, while within a week the *Coamo* would vanish as well.

CHAPTER 5

*. • • • • • • • • •

LOST IN THE FOG

Two of the crew of the schooner *Marathon* of Gloucester, George M. Roberts of Yarmouth, Nova Scotia, and James
Austin of Liverpool, Nova Scotia, left that vessel on the
Grand Banks at half past four in the afternoon of October 7,
1874, to visit their trawls. Soon after, a breeze came up and
a thick fog shut in. A dory, in which were two of the crew,
was paid out from the vessel to their assistance, but the warp
proved too short, and the fog became so thick that they soon
lost sight of each other.

They could hear the shouts of their companions, but all
efforts to reach them proved unavailing. It soon began to
rain, and the two men made up their minds to do the best
they could through the night, in hopes of finding their vessel
in the morning. Fortunately there were three trawl tubs on
board, and two of these were made fast to the painter * of
the dory, and did most excellent service as drogues, or sea
anchors, keeping her head to the sea.

The night passed drearily, and they were glad enough
when morning dawned. As the fog still enveloped them, they
rowed to the westward. It cleared up occasionally, but they
saw no vessel, and night came on again.

* Line or rope connected to the bow of the dory.

The next day was also foggy, and they laid to the drogue all day, drifting to the eastward. They took turns watching that night, hoping to catch a glimpse of some light from a passing vessel, but they were disappointed. It rained during the night, and they were fortunate enough to catch a good supply of water in their remaining tub; of this they drank sparingly, and it served to appease the fearful pangs of thirst and hunger.

On the third day they rowed to the northwest hoping to get into the track of the steamers. The fog still continued and no vessel was seen. They passed another night in suspense. The men were by this time discouraged, especially Mr. Austin, who had contracted a severe cold the first night out and was troubled with such severe shaking of his limbs that he could not sleep.

The morning of the fourth day was clear. The weather continued moderate through the day and this gave them courage. Although quite weak, they rowed to the westward, keeping an anxious lookout for some welcome sail, and doing their best to keep up each other's courage. A shark came alongside during the day and they endeavored to catch him, as they would gladly have partaken of anything edible, but were unsuccessful.

When the sun went down that night, the poor fellows felt their hearts sink within them. They thought their chances of being picked up were rather slim. Roberts was able to pass some of the weary hours in sleep, but this boon, for the most part, was denied his companion.

The fifth day was foggy. They rowed a couple of hours, but felt so used up that they gave up pulling, and another dreary night dragged its slow hours along. The sixth day they let the dory drift. During this time they saw the sun once or twice, but no vessel of any type came near them. The night shut down again, bringing terrible discouragement.

The seventh day was foggy. Strange to say, the fog revived them, and they cheered up. They drank sparingly from the tiny water supply, and apparently it satisfied their hunger as well. Shortly after this they agreed to start rowing again, and by afternoon had covered an estimated three miles to the north. Then they let the dory drift.

Now an intense longing to be rescued from the boat dominated all their thoughts. For the eighth time the sun went down and still there were no signs of relief. They watched eagerly through the early evening hours, and both came to realize that they could not hold out much longer. They talked of their chances as men will talk when in the face of a common danger, and both were of the opinion that another twenty-four hours would find them dead. They then lay down. Both men, in the silent depths of their hearts, prayed most fervently that they might be picked up before morning.

Soon after, Roberts thought he heard the noise of a steamer and raised his head above the side of the dory. To their unspeakable joy, a steamer's lights appeared not fifty yards distant. The dory had been seen from her deck, and the shouts of the men were soon answered. Roberts was enabled to get on board without help, but it required the assistance of two of the steamer's crew to get Austin on board.

The rescue craft proved to be the ocean steamer *Greece*. The fishermen were well cared for by her captain and officers, and by careful nursing were almost fully recovered when the *Greece* arrived in New York. Upon leaving the steamer, the men were presented with twenty dollars each, a gift from her officers and passengers.

An extremely singular circumstance connected with their affair is that at nine o'clock that evening the captain of the steamer altered his course half a point to the northward. If he had not done so, he would have gone so far to the southward as not to have seen the dory, and in all probability the two men would have perished. A kind Providence had ordered it otherwise. Their prayers were heard, and from the dangers which surrounded them they were returned to their friends.

CHAPTER 6

• • • • • • • • • •

JACK BUNKER

One of the forgotten legends of the Revolution concerns a man by the picturesque name of Jack Bunker. It was told to Mary Bradford Crowninshield in the year 1886 by Mate Antony Guptil of Mount Desert Island. Not until the summer of 1967 was the story confirmed. As a boy Guptil had obtained the story from his grandfather.

As a child Mary Crowninshield had been lucky enough to take a trip aboard the lighthouse tender *Iris*. In the book *All Among the Lighthouses,* which she later wrote, she changed the name of the tender to *Goldenrod,* and did not call the captain by his right name, probably because the Government would not allow it. My research indicates that the captain of the *Iris* was Edward W. Johnson.

One day when the lighthouse tender was near the western side of Somes Sound on Mount Desert Island, the passengers noticed a grassy slope between the cliffs and the shore on the western side of the sound. The captain identified the location as Norwood's Cove, and explained that Norwood's Cove was the place where Jack Bunker, during the Revolution, actually brought a British craft from Wiscasset, Maine.

At the height of the Revolution, the people of Mount Desert were almost starving to death. Jack had heard that the craft in question was collecting provisions for the English troops, and the last anyone had heard from her, she was operating in the "Sheepscote" River. Jack was then in his prime. He went to his sister's house to see how they were getting along with so little food.

"Poorly," was her answer.

"And you are almost tuckered out yourself, isn't that so, Hannah?"

Hannah began to cry, and Jack told her to keep up her spirits as he was going to see that she had enough food within the week, and some to spare.

As the weather was relatively good, Jack Bunker put his canoe into the sea at Somes Sound and headed straight down the coast for the Sheepscot River, with only one man as a bow paddler with him. The neighbors who watched him go by wondered what "wild Jack" was after, but they had their own troubles of hunger and thought no more of it.

Let us ask Mary Crowninshield to tell us what happened then. She quotes the language of her friend Mate Antony Guptil, who had fifty-three years in the lighthouse service:

"So Jack Bunker paddled out near Greening's Island and into the Western Passage, and headed as near as he could for Owl's Head; through the Thoroughfares he went, and down the coast of Maine until he came to the Sheepscot River.

"And paddling along up toward Wiscasset, lyin' by late one afternoon until it got dark enough, he came up softly to the vessel he was after. Not a sound came from on board. Jack paddled up under the bows, and listened. Nothin' to be heard but the lap-lap-lappin' of the tide and the stream as they was a-rushin' outward bound to the eternal ocean; nothin' to be seen but the black hulk and blacker water, an' a star now an' then shinin' overhead: fer my gran'ther sayed —and I tell ye the tale as it was told to me—that every thing was in Jack Bunker's favor, and that the clouds was a-flittin' eastward, blowing a reg'lar hurricane up aloft, and promisin' a fine fair wind fer the trip right down the coast.

"Wall, Children, thar was the Britisher, an' thar was Jack Bunker, an' silence reigned in the vessel. Lookin' shoreward, Jack see a house where there was lights, and revelry by night, an' all the rest of it; an' he come to the conclusion, did Jack, thet there was a party ashore, an' that they hed up and gone, an' hedn't left no one to welcome strangers. Jack clim up the forrad chains; silence grew putty decided; then he tip-toed aft, quite soft an' easy; silence got louder an' more plain; an', seein' no lights nor nothin', he soon came to the opinion that his summises hed been corect,—thet the vessel was hisn, an' thet all he had to do was to get away with her: so he called soft-like to his mate. They h'isted the canoe aboard, cut the cable, h'sted the jib, an' made sail; an', with the wind a-blowing' all the guns in England on the starboard beam, they stood down the river, an' was before long in blue water; an' then they give her her head, an' away she went, lickety split, like a scalded cat: an' next day she rounded to Norwood's Cove.

" 'Come down here, all of ye,' said Jack, 'fer there's enough an' to spare'; an' down they come, an' they took enough out o' thet schooner to last 'em for months to come. An' then old Jack got under way, fer he expected to be chased, an' chased he was; but she was a fast sailer, if she was a Britisher, an' he ran her down to Roque Island,—commonly called Rogue Island, ye know, sir,' looking at the inspector: 'an' the place where he run in is called Bunker's Hole to this day.

" 'They cut away her masts, cut down trees an' laid 'em across to hide her, an' her old hulk was there for years an' years. I'll show ye the place, children, if I live out this trip.' "

It is said that Jack Bunker buried the strong box of the British craft in the area near Bunker's Cove. It has never been found, but on our trip to Bunker's Cove in 1967 we did see a substantial collection of money buried in earth and leaves within a short distance of the Cove itself. As there may be another sizable amount there, I have promised not to reveal any more information.

Jack Bunker himself is buried on one of the Cranberry Islands.

Whether or not Mate Antony Guptil was ever able to carry out his promise and show the children Bunker's Hole and Bunker's Cove, as the Government chart calls them today, I probably will never discover.

CHAPTER 7

. . . .

JEREMIAH BUMSTEAD

One of my earliest thrills, now approaching sixty years ago, was in accompanying my grandmother Caroline Keating Rowe to the Old State House in Boston to read through the great masses of reference works and scrapbooks which are still available there. Grandmother was one of the first students at Wheaton College in Norton, Massachusetts, before it was a college, and during a period when it was considered unusual for a woman to go to a seminary or college at all. I recall my first surprise during one of my Old State House visits on reading of the pirate Captain Phillips, whose head was preserved in a pickle barrel along with the head of one of his sailors.

Old documents still fascinate me. Recently it has been my pleasure to obtain a copy of the entire known diary of Jeremiah Bumstead of Boston. His descendant, Harlow Hardinge, who lives in York, Pennsylvania, became aware of Bumstead's many activities through the perusal of this diary. Indeed it is an unusual one, for it was written on the margins and blank spaces in a series of early almanacs. Because of the efforts, more than a century ago, of Samuel Foster Haven, I am able to include portions of the diary in this chapter.[*]

[*] A copy of the diary was printed in July 1861 in the *New England Historical and Genealogical Register* edited by Mr. Haven.

Jeremiah Bumstead kept the diary from 1722 to 1727. He was a staunch, active member of the Old South Church. Not ambitious for high office, when he was chosen constable Bumstead paid a fine and obtained his release by pleading that he had "no hand except his own." The items of his unusual diary which interest me I include in this chapter in italics.

1722

June 12.   Ye Privateer, Popillin,* went after ye piratt.
July 23.   6 Indians, taken att Dunstable, brought into Boston.

I find no other mention of Indians being taken this year at Dunstable, but only a few days before this the red men began to attack the people in the eastern areas. On the twenty-fifth of July, war was proclaimed by the government of Massachusetts against "the Eastern Indians and their Confederates." These Indians were probably seized to prevent their joining the enemy.

July 25.   15 more [Indians] brought in from Nashaway.
July 26.   War proclaimed against ye Indians. I paid to James Franklin 7 pound for 5 hundred of Mr. Vincents 3 Sermons on forgiveness.

Thomas Vincent was "sometimes Minister of Maudlin Milk-street in London." His books include *An Explicatory Catechism: or, an Explanation of the Assemblies Shorter Catechism,* and the imprint runs: *"Boston in New England:* Printed for *D. Henchman,* over against the Brick-Meeting-house in Cornhill, *John Phillips,* at the Stationer's-Arms, and *T. Hancock,* at the Bible and Three Crowns near the Town-Dock, 1729." Mr. Vincent appears to have been very popular with the immediate descendants of the Puritans.

---

* The name of the privateer captain was Peter Papillon.

September 24. Dr. Perkins drowned in ye mill creek. Train-
ing day I mended or graffted on a peece on ye top of ye Ensign's
staff, & rivitted ye spear on again, & stained it for ye company—
worth 2–6.
October 30. On ye last day of October a Scooner* burnt
at ye end of ye long wharff, & a man burnt in her.

"Last week one of the Chiefs of the Mohawks lately come to
town, died at the Royal Exchange Tavern in King street, and
was magnificently interred on Friday night last. A drawn sword
lay on the coffin, and the Pall was supported by six Captains of
the militia. The gentlemen of the Council followed next the
corps, and then the Justices of the Town and the commission
Officers of the Militia. At last followed four Indians, the two
hindmost (whom the government had appointed to attend him
in his sickness) with each a pappoos at her back." New England
Courant, 22 Oct. 1722.

1723

February 24. Great storm of wind and haill; wind att north,
ye tide rises in Union Street as high up as Mr. Hunt's house—
in ye Middle of ye street—to ye filling many sellers and loss of
abundance of treasure, & spoyling a great deal more.

This was one of the four great New England hurricanes.
The others occurred in 1635, 1815, and 1938.

March 30. On ye 30th, about 5 o'clock in ye morning, a fier
in Dr. Cook's buildings, near ye long wharf,—7 or 8 tenements
burnt out, as Mr. Buttlop, Salter, Man, Mayo, & others.
May 10. Mr. Scutts came home from England & brought me
files for a piece of eight, 14½ cc & ½ hand saw.

It was common custom to file off slivers of coins and melt
them, thus "files for a piece of eight." This eventually led to
milled edges on coins to detect this habit.

---

* *Scooner* is an early mention of a vessel of the name. See Babson's *History*
of Gloucester for an interesting account of the origin of such vessels.

May 30. Singing lecture Dr. Cotton Mather preached ye 2d time att that lecture.

July 4. Ye negro Dago hanged for fiering Mr. Powell's house, & Mr. Cooper preacht ye lecture on that occation, from Job 7 & 20.

*July 19. 26 pirattes hanged at Roadiland, 2 reprieved for a year and 8 cleared.**

December 26. I received of Mr. Miers, at ye north, a Round piece of Spechelwood, about 12 foot long, & 3 inches through; and a piece of Redwood, 6 foot long and about 4 inches through.

1724

February 1. On ye 1. Mr. Valintine, ye lawyer, hanged himself, att home, in his upper chamber, with his sash. Mr. Harris, minister, & Mr. Auchmutty, giving oath of his distraction, he had a funerall, and was buryed in ye Church yard on ye 4 day of ye month.

May 3. On ye 3, ye pirate Sloope was brought in by some captive men that rose and tost ye master mate over board, & knocked down Phillips ye Capt., cutt of his head, & ye head of Burrill, having chapt him down with an ax, & the gunner with an adds. Phillip's & Burrill's heads were brought to Boston in pickle.†

June 2. On ye 2. Rose Archer, & White, 2 Piaratts hanged at ye ferry. Mr. Webb wallkt with them & prayed thare; their flagg was set on the gallows.

June 8. My wife & Jery & Betty, David Cunningham & his wife, & 6 more, went to ye castle to Governors Island, & to see ye piratte in Gibbits att Bird Island.

---

* Newport hanging. See my book *True Tales of Pirates and Their Gold*, and *R. I. Colonial Records* IV, 331. Mr. Bartlett, editor of that valuable work, has given the main facts in a note, relative to the pirates. Several who were hanged were from New England.

† My book *True Tales of Pirates and Their Gold* tells this story.

Bird Island was large when the country was first settled, and was so probably at this time, but seventy years later (1794) it had so worn away by the action of the currents, that it was only visible at low water. It has long since entirely disappeared. It was located about one mile from Long Wharf.

August 22. 28 Indian scalps brought to Boston; one of them was Bombazens, and one fryer Railes.

The scalps were the result of the expedition against Norridgewock under Colonel Moulton.

November 23. A great storm at S.E.; did a great deal of damage to ye vessels at ye Long wharff, in breaking their heads and starns.

November 24. News came this month of David Bassett's Death in ye West Indies. He & another. Their throats were cutt on board his vessel when asleep on ye hay on ye quarter deck, in ye day time, 17 August last.

1725

March 9. 10 Indians scallps brought in & in ye next month, April, 2 more Indians killed by a lad of 17 years of age & their scalps brought to town, & 25 pound in money paid him down, and ye remainder of ye 2 hundred put out to use for him by ye authority. Mr. Lovell was ye captain that brought in those 10 scalps, who afterwards was killed in another fight.

I was this month chose, ye 3d time, to ye office of a Tithingman.

May 8. Capt. Lovell and His lieutenant Farewell killed in a fight they had with ye Indians.

July 30. I went to Mr. Thatcher's of Milton. He then gave me 2 of Mr. Bailys allmanacks or Diarys for ye years 82 & 95. He then told me he was entered on ye 75th year of his age.

November 4. Captain Norris & Mr. Griddly returned home,

*having bin gone a fortnight in a boat designed for Manchester,
with 6 or 7 more persons, & narrowly scapt with their lives
near Barnstable. Paid Mr. Addison's score 1–12–7.*

*December 9. Old Mrs. Pollard buryed, aged 105. From ye
Courant No. 228—"Mrs. Ann Pollard, widow of Mr. William
Pollard, born at Saffron Walden in ye kingdom of England,
died Dec. 6, in ye 105th year of her age. She has left of her
offspring 130."*

1726

*January 6. A Brigantine from St. Christofers cast away near
Deer Island. All ye men lost, except ye master & boy.*

*May 13. Ye bones of a humane person found by one digging
clams in ye mill pond att low water mark against ye lower
end of Mr. Checkly's lane.*

May 19. One Miller drowned at pudden [Pullin?] point. A
1 handed man. Ye boat sunk, & 2 other men saved. Abigall
Wheeler dyed of a feaver, aged 19; & buryed on ye 22. Att ye
funerall 600 persons.*

*June 15. News from South Carolina of Fr. Holms senior's
death. I paid Mr. Chaffin for his caine 12s. Having putt on
a ivory head of mine 4 inches long, I sould it for 20.*

*June 28. A smart clap of thunder & lightning struck Elder
Limun's [Lyman's] house. 4 piratts brought in.*

*July 10. Mr. Sewall in ye forenoon preacht to 2 of ye pirattes,
(4 in all) viz., Henry Greenvil & George Candick, from those
words, Acts 17, 30, on repentance. In ye afternoon Saml Cole
went with them to Mr. Colman's church. He preacht from Heb.
10, 31. Capt. William Fly refused to go out till he went to ye
gallows. On ye 12, 3 were executed, viz., Fly, Quartermaster
Cole, & Henry Greenvil. George Candick was repreved from
ye gallows, & Capt. Fly hung up in chains at Mixes [Nix's] Mate.
3 ministers went to prayer with them, viz., Mr. Checkley, Mr.
Cotton, & Mr. Marshall of Brantry.*

July 11. A young woman—her name was Nowell, age 16, was

* Point Shirley Gut.

shott in ye head (she never spoke after) by a negro boy as she was looking out of a back upper chamber window, near ye sign of ye oringe tree. Buryed on ye 14 day.

July 14. Dr. Mather preacht a funerall sermon for Mrs. Cotton, Mr. Roland Cotton's widow, from Malachi 3 chap. & former part of ye 17 verse; Showing ye Riteous are Jewells. He read some part of her Diary, from her own paper & sung ye former part of ye 16 psalm. It being ye lecture after Capt. Fly was hanged, who I think may be reasoned an unparreled instance of a hard heart,* Ye Doctor, I suppose might think it enough to hint his name in ye psalm, not mentioning any thing of them or him, otherwise than in a holy scorn. Viz., "My lips their names shall Fly." *

August 15. Our Lieutenant Governer & Gentlemen & Soulders arrived here from Casco, having made a peace with ye Indians.

October 7. 2 young men drowned near ye south battery in a cannoo, viz., Saml. Day & a Jersey lad; & 2 negroes then saved, being 4 in all.

November 2. John Battis, a Frenchman, his son, & 3 Indians were hanged at Charlestown ferry. Mr. Sewall & Mr. Cooper prayed on ye stage. They were all cutt down & buryed at Bird-Island.

1727

May 16. Bought a pair of large coloured stockings, att Mr. Armstrongs, for 12s.

July 12. Ye North Mill struck with Thunder, ye miller Chiley & his son struck down.

Also Mr. Richard Flood, Currier, was drowned near Governors Island, about ye same time.

July 19. Mr. Adams, blockmaker, & his man dyed by ye vapor of Dr. Noyse's that was, his well—sliding down by a rope to lash ye lower peece of ye pump in order to histe it up.

September 16. A great storm at North.east, that did much

---

* See my *True Tales of Pirates and Their Gold.*

*damage in ye town, viz., by ye fall of a chimney Mrs. Sheaff's
child killed, & her leg broke.*

*October 29. Att better than an hour after ten a clock att
night, a very surprising Earth-Quake in Boston and ye Towns
round about. Dr. Mather had a full meeting at his church next
morning; & Mr. Sewall & Mr. Foxcrafft att their churches next
night by candlelight, for prayer & preaching.*

The earthquake of 1727 is called by Sidney Perley "the
greatest" that New England has probably experienced since
its settlement. At the time a report came that the Blue Hills
had "sunk!"

A Nantucket fisherman hastily launched his boat when the
quake hit, afraid that the island would sink.

At Newbury more than ten chasms opened up a foot or
more in width, while near Spring Island sixteen to twenty
loads of sulfurous sand were thrown up.

The clergy called the earthquake a "loud call to the whole
land to repent and fear and give glory to God."

In Salem after the earthquake all records were broken for
church service attendance, with the "upper meeting House"
jammed to capacity by the largest congregation "ever in that
edifice."

Whether or not Bumstead wrote other diaries, it is believed
those at the New England Historic Genealogical Society are
the only ones which have been preserved.

CHAPTER 8

. . . .

FAR-FLUNG BOON ISLAND

Among the treasures I have saved since the earliest years of my interest in New England is a letter written by the man whose career is associated more than that of anyone else with isolated Boon Island, located off the Maine Coast. His name is William W. Williams.

Long ago he told me of early Boon Island history. Incidentally, the shipwreck which gave Boon Island its name occurred at least before the 1675 King Phillip's War, for when John Sellers made his New England chart-map in that period, he included Boon Island by name on the document. We know today that it was a wreck of one and possibly two craft which caused the residents of the area to make plans for shipwrecked survivors stranded on the island.

Keeper Williams explained how a " 'boon' or barrel of provisions was kept on the rock from the latter part of the seventeenth century until the light was established." The food was brought out by the fishermen from the York area, and in following this custom from year to year the fishermen gave the ledge the name "Boon Island."

The tall shaft at Boon Island was erected at the instigation of General Benjamin Lincoln, who in 1811 wrote to Albert Gallatin, Secretary of the Treasury, that it "does not appear that the sea ever makes a breach over the island." Lincoln must have forgotten that the beacon had been washed away in the great storm of 1804 when the great billows completely engulfed Boon Island. The lighthouse was finished in 1811, the same year in which Lincoln wrote his letter.

Captain Williams writes that the most exciting time he ever had at Boon Island Light was the rescue of a crew from the schooner *Goldhunter*.

"It was the coldest morning I had ever seen so early in December," wrote Captain Williams. "The thermometer was four below zero, and it was a thick vapor, and blowing a gale of wind from the northwest. The schooner struck off Boon Island Ledge * easterly of the station. Successful in getting into their yawl boat, the men reached the light station after a six hour row. It was then one-thirty in the morning.

"We were awakened by the barking of a dog, of all things, and this was the first notification we had that there were people around the island. Getting out our lanterns, we climbed down over the frozen rocks and soon saw the little boat just outside the breakers. We shouted to the men to follow the light around the rocks to the lee of the island, then, guided by the lanterns, make for the shore on the top of a sea. All this time we could hear the barking dog.

"When the boat came closer, we watched as the dog leaped into the water with the painter in his teeth, scrambled and skidded ashore over the ice to present that bow line to us. We pulled and slid the little craft up over the ice-covered rocks until we had it above the reach of the tide.

"The crew members were almost helpless, frozen as they were to the thwarts. Getting them out of the boat was hard enough, but the most difficult task was carrying them inside and bringing them back to life. I recall the fourteen-year-old

* Located two and three-quarter nautical miles east from Boon Island.

Negro boy who was terribly ill from exposure, and it was some time before we brought him around.*

"In the early days we communicated quite a lot by carrier pigeon, especially if there was a serious emergency. The fastest time of the pigeons, I believe, was exactly ten minutes from mainland to the light.

"I recall with pleasure the Thanksgiving when we really were rewarded by a miracle. There had been storm after storm at the station that November month, and we finally realized that we were not to get ashore to replenish our larder and therefore would have slim pickings for Thanksgiving itself.

"On Thanksgiving eve I was talking with the other men. We were pretending that we'd still enjoy Thanksgiving with hardtack and water, when suddenly the three of us heard a terrific blow or thud far up in the lighthouse, followed by another and still another. Climbing the tower, I reached the parapet deck, where I saw lying there four black ducks dead as a door nail. Later I found several more dead ducks, and indeed we really had a joyous and giant duck dinner the next afternoon, Thanksgiving.

"The ducks, of course, had been blinded by the bright beams of the lighthouse and had flown to their death by crashing against the panes of glass surrounding the lens.

"All my family ashore wondered how we fared that Thanksgiving, as they knew no lighthouse tender had been able to reach us with food. They didn't find out until after Christmas, when the *Myrtle* returned to land after bringing us our supplies just before the holiday.

"Without question Boon Island is one of the most barren places on the Maine Coast. Not one part of its several rocky acres is more than ten feet above high water mark, and there

---

* More than a quarter century later Keeper Williams met the boy, and they exchanged their recollections of the disaster which befell the *Goldhunter*.

isn't any natural soil at all. When I first went out to the island we carried dirt off in boxes and barrels so that at least we could have a small flower garden. Unhappily a good storm sweeps the flowers and the dirt right out to sea. I didn't mind it myself but for the poor children who were with us during the summer vacation months it made a big difference."

In my volume *The Fury of the Seas* I tell the story of how in 1711 Captain Dean ran his vessel, the *Nottingham Galley,* ashore at Boon Island and how cannibalism was necessary for the men to keep alive before they were rescued.

On Friday, February 11, 1944, the 7244-ton British freighter *Empire Knight* was proceeding in a bad snowstorm toward her wartime destination. Soon the captain found himself lost in the storm, and at 2:23 P.M. the heavily laden craft smashed up on Boon Island Ledge.

Because of war supplies aboard, the captain and crew remained on the doomed freighter in an attempt to save her. All that bitter afternoon mountainous waves swept over the *Empire Knight,* the icy water freezing the lifeboat falls and coating the entire vessel with a thick white sheathing.

With the coming of dawn the master realized that the freighter's position was impossible, so he ordered all hands to abandon ship. One lifeboat with three men aboard was lowered into the rough seas, but went over at once, throwing the men into the ocean. Two of the victims were soon hauled aboard a waiting rescue vessel. The third was unable to help himself. Several sailors went over the side and saved the seaman's life, swimming back to the vessel with him.

At eight-thirty the great freighter cracked in two between the saloon and the number three hatch. The bow section started to drift in a northerly direction but swung around and grounded again. As the giant waves battered the stern, it slid off with over a score of men aboard and disappeared in deep water, with almost all on the stern losing their lives. For miles around, the ocean was full of flotsam, and it is said that a Gloucester trawler salvaged much material, including giant bundles of auto tires.

In all, the rescue ships picked up twenty survivors, the Coast Guardsmen performing heroic feats in the freezing seas. Many of the sailors, however, had clung to the debris until their strength failed them and finally slipped off the wreckage to their deaths. In all, twenty-four sailors were lost. Fourteen bodies were eventually recovered and brought to Portsmouth, where a full military funeral was held a few days later. The twenty survivors attended the final rites for their dead comrades. Fourteen women of the same nationalities as the dead sailors acted as mother-mourners, and later wrote letters to the next of kin of the men who perished.

The Massachusetts Marine Historical League visited the cemetery in 1960. Miss Marie Hansen of the League, of Danish blood as were most of the victims, represented the women from overseas whose loved ones were buried so far from their native land.

In the 1870s Keeper Edwin Hobbs was in charge at Boon Island Light. A diary loaned to me by his relation, Stillman Hobbs of Hampton, New Hampshire, tells of an unhappy existence out at Boon Island when families were allowed to live there. As there is no way to interpret the various items in the record, I offer them without comment.

Boon Island 1874
July
22nd   Mrs. White choked my little girl this day
30th   She thretened to tie my girls hands and throw her into the sea

Aug
12th   Mrs. White took eggs from my hen roost this day
16th   She thretened my girls life in the boat house this day

18th   She told me a falshood in regard to looking after the oil.
" "   Mr. White told me to day Mr. Card took from this sta-
        tion two barrils of coal belonging to the station also oil
        at sundry times.

Boon Island Aug 27th 1874
Mrs. White made threts to my girl to day. Thretened to take
her life also she would Kick and strike her any time she saw fit.
Also called me a liar and I could prove it by Mr. White, John
Glen and others.

Jan. Tuesday 26th 1875
The Tower caught a fire in the morning during, or after Mr.
Whites watch, he haveing the last watch.

Oct. 1st 1875
Mr. Leavitt & Mr. White had quite a number of hard words,
in the which Mr. White called Mr. Leavitt hard names called
him an Gord Damed him all up in a heep.

1876
Oct. 29	Mr. White commenced boarding with me this day at two dollars per week. 2.00	
	Went in Nov 19 making three weeks amt	6.00
Nov. 26	Came back Sunday	
	Went in Jan 6 taking out six weeks for board	12.00
	Paid	$18.00

Jan. 12th	Returned Jan 12	
Feb. 2d	Went in Feb 2d making 3 weeks	6.00
	Returned Feb 6	
	Went in March 5th making 4 weeks	8.00

Fish sold from Boon Island
To William Downs & son
130 large Cod 8 cts	10.40	
78 Small Cod 5 cts	3.90	
	14.30	

Celia Thaxter, who is associated with the Isles of Shoals, wrote of a terrible event at Boon Island Light. Mrs. Thaxter tells us that "two lovers lately wed" went out to run the lighthouse at Boon Island. At the beginning of the winter, as far as can be recalled, the husband was killed in a great storm and the unhappy woman kept the light burning for the next three nights until the storm went down. Then, to attract attention to her terrible plight, she left the light in darkness so that she might get help.

Excerpts from *The Watch of Boon Island* by this gifted Isles of Shoals poet, Celia Thaxter, follow.

They crossed the lonely and lamenting sea;
　　Its moaning seemed but singing. "Wilt thou dare,"
He asked her, "brave the loneliness with me?"
　　"What loneliness," she said, "if thou art there?"

Afar and cold on the horizon's rim
　　Loomed the tall lighthouse, like a ghostly sign;
They sighed not as the shore behind grew dim,—
　　A rose of joy they bore across the brine.

They gained the barren rock, and made their home
　　Among the wild waves and the sea-birds wild.
The wintry winds blew fierce across the foam;
　　But in each other's eyes they looked and smiled.

Death found them; turned his face and passed her by,
　　But laid a finger on her lover's lips;
And there was silence. Then the storm ran high,
　　And tossed and troubled sore the distant ships.

Three times the night, too terrible to bear,
　　Descended, shrouded in the storm. At last

The sun rose clear and still on her despair,
  And all her striving to the winds she cast,

And bowed her head, and let the light die out,
  For the wide sea lay calm as her dead love.
When evening fell, from the far land, in doubt,
  Vainly to find that faithful star men strove.

. . .

Out from the coast toward her high tower they sailed;
  They found her watching, silent, by her dead,—
A shadowy woman, who nor wept nor wailed,
  But answered what they spake, till all was said.

CHAPTER 9

· · · · · · · · · ·

THE SUBCHASER *S-241*

Shortly before noon on July 1, 1918, the subchaser *S-241*, cruising in waters of the North Atlantic off Nova Scotia, sighted a German submarine on her starboard side. It was extremely foggy with visibility less than two hundred yards. At three-forty that afternoon, the commander of the *S-241* spotted a torpedo heading for a nearby freighter, but the freighter was able to maneuver and escape.

Five minutes later the *S-241* came up with a U-boat, which was off the starboard quarter, running on a parallel course with her periscope two feet above the surface of the sea, and proceeding at a speed of seven knots.

Then came the moment of action. When the submarine was less than thirty-five yards away, the order came for depth charges to be fired from the Y gun.* One charge landed in perfect position ten yards ahead of the periscope, which vanished immediately. Five seconds later there was a terrific explosion, and the surrounding waters clearly indicated the destruction of the German submarine.

---

* Mounted on the stern, the Y gun is an antisubmarine gun with two barrels which form a fork in the shape of a Y. It is used to project simultaneously a depth charge on each side of the vessel on which the gun is mounted.

All of the above, without question, is a far cry from a hike I took out on the frozen marsh in back of our residence on February 27, 1968, but there is a connection, for out on what is known as the Hanover Flats between Humarock and Marshfield rest the remains of the famous *S-241* which sank that U-boat fifty years ago.

Indeed, it has taken me many years to line up all the items for the complete story, but now in this chapter I present the saga of the *S-241*.

Ever since the Snow family moved to Marshfield, and the number of years is gradually approaching two decades, I had been told conflicting stories of the history of the fascinating wreck which lies on the southern slope of Hanover Flats in what is now called the South River.

The wreck, which is identified for the first time on the government North River chart, lies between Fourth Cliff in Scituate and the entrance to Branch Creek, Marshfield.

The first story I heard about the craft was that she had been a rumrunner trapped and abandoned under heavy gunfire on Hanover Flats during prohibition days.

Then I learned that the vessel was not a rumrunner, but a rum chaser * which, after a successful career, ended her days on the edge of the North River, going ashore on Hanover Flats in a gale.

A prominent resident of the area objected to this story, telling me that the craft was originally neither a rumrunner nor a rum chaser, but actually a submarine chaser which had been converted into a rumrunner during prohibition and operated in the Marshfield-Scituate area for three years. During this time its owner is said to have buried hundreds of

---

* A rumrunner was a boat carrying illegal liquor during the prohibition era, while a rum chaser was a government craft that attempted to capture the rumrunner.

cases of liquor in the area. I visited two of the cache sites with John Eames of Marshfield, and surely enough, it did appear as though something bulky had been placed in each location at some time in the past.

Another visitor to the flats assured me that scores of bottles had been hastily pushed into the soft ooze of the marsh and were still there. As to whether or not the contents were usable, he did not offer any comment.

Not too long ago another story reached me. The wreck had been a submarine chaser, and was sold as surplus to a gentleman who was in the postal service and whose descendants still live in Marshfield.

Year after year stories have been told of the craft, but always the elusive facts necessary for accurate recording have just escaped me. Then during the summer of 1966 the government decided to survey the entrance to the North and South rivers.

Our New England hurricanes are responsible for the present shape of the North River shore line. Until the storm of 1635 the river mouth was located where it is today, but on August 15 of that year the first of the four great New England hurricanes hit the coast, sealing the mouth completely and opening a new exit several miles to the south, not too far from the place where the southernmost of the two Humarock bridges now crosses the South River.

The Portland Gale of November 1898 broke through the old mouth of the river and sealed up the newer mouth to the south, making the North River the South River up to the break-through. The North River retained its name from the break-through between the Third and Fourth cliffs all the way up to its source.

Whether the new survey of 1966 was prompted by the many relatively recent accidents and drownings at the mouth of the river, I do not know, but indeed the survey was sorely needed.

George Moore, chief of the local Boston office of the U. S. Coast and Geodetic Survey, informed me in the summer of 1966 that his men were to set up headquarters in a portable office at the Simms Boatyard in Scituate, comfortably close to the mouth of the river.*

When I first visited their trailer, the government men conversed with me in terms of mean low water, boat sheets, and tidal reducers, while I countered with tales of various wrecks in the area, including the *Helena,* the *Puritan,* the *Pinthis,* the alleged Norse galleon, and the grindstone schooner.†

The survey was finished that autumn and the new North River Chart which accompanies Coast and Geodetic Survey 1207 was published.

The mysterious subchaser wreck which has so many divergent stories connected with it is located on the new Correction to Chart 1207. Those who have the new chart will also find three other locations of wrecks. ‡ One is in the North River not too far from Damon's Point, while the other two are in the Herring River on the way up to Greenbush. §

The publication of the first real chart ever made of the area between my Marshfield residence and the mouth of the North-South River gave me the extra impetus needed to begin an all-out effort to locate once and for all someone who knew the facts about what had become a mystery craft.

Finally, with the help of several residents of Marshfield who prefer to remain anonymous, I obtained the name of

* The survey was made by Lieutenant G. M. Wood, Ensign Richard F. Coons, R. B. Wilson, F. S. Brown, J. H. Rice, and W. E. Cason.

† The grindstone schooner was lost in 1830, the *Puritan* in 1896, the *Helena* in 1909, and the *Pinthis* in 1930. The last person to recover a grindstone from the 1830 wreck of the schooner was Donald Hourihan in 1967.

‡ These wrecks are all schooners, as yet unidentified.

§ The Herring River starts near the Scituate Tennis Club of Greenbush and flows into the North River near Wills Island.

Mrs. Dorothy Johnson, and it was she who solved the mystery. Thus I am able now to tell the true story of submarine chaser *241*, including her career in the First World War.

Submarine Chaser *S-241* had a normal displacement of 77 tons, with a full load displacement of 85 tons. Her length between perpendiculars was 105 feet, with her overall length 110 feet. She was built by the New York Launch and Engine Company at Morris Heights, New York, at a cost of $72,600 in 1918.

She drew five and one-half feet and her highest speed on trial was 18 knots. Her battery consisted of one three-inch gun, two machine guns, and one Y gun. She had three propellers, three standard gas engines, and a complement of twenty-seven men, two of whom were wardroom officers and one a chief petty officer.

Her captain at the time of commissioning on April 8, 1918, was Ensign Robert L. Mills.* Unfortunately, after casting off, she hit a submerged log in the East River while under the Brooklyn Bridge, but evidently this accident caused little damage.

Two days later she helped put out a fire on her sister craft, the *S-247*, and then got under way for New London, Connecticut, where she docked at the State Pier. She received submarine detectors and wireless telephone apparatus and on May 13 left New London for Halifax, Nova Scotia, where five days later she was put through the usual inspection by an admiral in the British navy and the following week was moored alongside the destroyer U.S.S. *DeLong* at the Halifax Naval Dock.

During the following week she operated in and around Halifax as dispatch, mail, and guard boat, and also did patrol

---

* On May 4, 1918, her ammunition was put aboard from Submarine Chaser *S-165* and the next day 390 gallons of gas were placed aboard.

duty. Her most exciting day, July 1, 1918, I have already described, and her history continues from that point.

Her destruction of the U-boat completed, Subchaser *241* swung around, headed for Nova Scotia, and eventually reached Halifax. It is not known whether the U-boat destroyed by the *S-241* was ever identified, but it was one of a fleet operating off our continent.

The war came to an end. The submarine chaser was sold as surplus material on May 11, 1921, to John F. Smith, Dorothy Smith Johnson's father. With her engine room completely stripped, the craft came down from Boston by tug and was anchored in the river. For the next few years there were glorious times enjoyed aboard the *S-241*. The family painted the entire interior in complementary harmony, but what the young people especially enjoyed were relatively rare visits to the crow's-nest and pilothouse.

Then came a storm in November 1925. At the height of the gale the chaser broke away from her mooring and was pushed across to Hanover Flats, where she grounded and soon went over on her beam ends. The bow fetched up heading toward Third Cliff.

Deciding to secure her permanently to the marshland in the manner of a pier or wharf, they sank poles into the semisolid marsh. Holes were then drilled into the hull of the boat, and as the tide came in the water filled the subchaser so that she slowly fitted into the pierlike framework.

The following spring the Smiths went down to the *S-241* and removed the pilothouse and crow's-nest.

At this time John Smith, Mrs. Johnson's father, worked for the West Somerville Post Office. Each year the family came down by cabin cruiser from the Mystic Lakes in Medford, through the Mystic River, making the entire journey by sea down to the North River mouth.

It was the custom for eight or ten families to camp in tents on the lee side of Humarock Beach between Hatch's Boatyard and the Fourth Cliff. There were no people there until after the First World War, and the famous Fourth Cliff Life Saving Station was a lonely sentinel.

After enduring two or three bad storms, the group decided they had to put up something more substantial than a tent, and there was the *S-241* to be utilized. Eventually, after much planning, the Smiths built a six-room house on the deck of the *S-241*.

Now that the family had moved aboard the subchaser, happy days were many. At almost every low tide in the summer the members of the Smith clan would go clam digging. They would have contests between the different families of the area to see who could dig the most clams. Dorothy Smith Johnson became quite a digger and remembers the local fishermen paying her one dollar for every bushel she dug.

They would go up under the bridge to get their water at a spring where Royal Brown's place is located today.

Earl James Johnson now entered the picture. His family lived in the Brockton area. One day he noticed the tents and the boat and went down to investigate. He began the habit of coming over and visiting the Smith family, and engaged Dorothy in conversation. Soon they became seriously interested in each other, and their marriage came some time later.

John Smith retired from the post office around 1934, eventually selling the subchaser. Around 1943 there was a bad fire on the *S-241*. The fire department could not send any apparatus out to the blaze, and the *S-241* burned to the water's edge in spectacular fashion.

On Monday, July 1, 1968, the fiftieth anniversary of the *S-241*'s proudest moment, a small group from the Massachusetts Marine Historical League visited what remained of the craft out on Hanover Flats. After a brief ceremony the members paid their respects to the crew of the *S-241* who had achieved fame half a century before far out on the rough waters of the North Atlantic when they sent a German submarine to the bottom.

CHAPTER 10

. . . .

THE *PORTLAND*

The loss of the steamer *Portland* was one of the most unusual and tragic disasters ever to hit New England. The 291-foot steamer *Portland,* a paddle-wheeler designed by William F. Pattee, was built at the Bath, Maine, shipyard and was launched with appropriate ceremonies on October 11, 1889. Seaworthy and of great strength, she was one of the outstanding craft of her day. Whenever she appeared along the New England coast everyone paused to watch with delight the white and gold-trimmed steamer with her truly beautiful lines. Many believed it an honor and privilege to take passage on the *Portland,* as she was noted for her exquisite furnishings, courteous waiters and stewards, and luxurious appointments.

For some time, in answer to scores upon scores of requests, I have been compiling an entire book concerned with the *Portland* disaster. Nevertheless, the years are passing, and as there are so many items never revealed before in my other books, it is not fair to hold them indefinitely. Therefore I include them in this chapter. The entire volume on the *Portland* must await the time when all those who are aiding me

in various parts of New England have completed their individual research efforts.

When the first chilling winds of a piercing November gale
come swirling into the harbors and inlets along the New
England coast, there are gray, aging mariners who recall the
terrific hurricane of November 1898. Regardless of the hundreds of other vessels sunk or wrecked during this violent
tempest, mention of the gale usually brings to the minds of
New England inhabitants one outstanding event—the loss of
the steamer *Portland*. Although seventy years have elapsed
since the momentous night when she steamed out to meet the
hurricane which proved her doom, there are still a few mariners who vividly recall the famous vessel which gave her
name to that storm. Many controversial stories have been advanced through the years concerning the fate of this handsome steamer, and it is probable that the complete story of
the *Portland* will never be known.

There has always been a heated argument as to whether
or not Captain Hollis H. Blanchard of the *Portland* was ordered to sail from Boston that night. When I interviewed Miss
Grace Blanchard, granddaughter of the captain, she told me
that her father, Charles Blanchard, visited the captain shortly
before the *Portland* sailed.

"My father asked my grandfather if it was necessary for him
to sail," explained Miss Blanchard. "Grandfather Blanchard
said to his son, 'I have my orders to sail, and I am going!'
Those were the last words ever spoken by my grandfather to
a member of the family."

At precisely seven o'clock that night the final departing
whistle from the *Portland* split the chill night air of Boston's
Atlantic Avenue, and Captain Hollis Blanchard sailed into
the unknown. Since November 26, 1898, was the Saturday
after Thanksgiving, there were more passengers than usual

returning to Maine after spending the holiday with relatives in the Boston area or Philadelphia or even farther south.

Some people have believed that the *Portland* was not seen after leaving Boston, but this is simply not so. Captain William Thomas of Bailey Island, Maine, of the fishing craft *Maud S.*, saw the *Portland* when he was nearly four miles southwest of Thacher's Island. Captain Lynes B. Hathaway of Brockton saw her as she slid by Thacher's Island at 9:30 P.M. and at eleven o'clock Captain Reuben Cameron of the *Grayling* sighted her twelve miles south by east of Thacher's. At 11:15 P.M. Captain Frank Stream passed her in the area, and at 11:45 P.M. Captain D. J. Pellier of the *Edgar Randall* also sighted her, with Eastern Point fourteen miles away, southeast by east.*

Meanwhile the storm had become a hurricane. In Boston gusts up to seventy-two knots were registered, and shipping everywhere scurried to safety.

It is possible and even probable that the *Portland* began shipping seas soon after she headed for the open ocean in order to attempt to ride out the gale. Captain Blanchard had successfully done this before under similar circumstances. It is believed that the steamer soon began listing to starboard, forcing her port paddle wheel out of the water, while the starboard wheel was still turning. Heading toward the open sea, Captain Blanchard could not offset the drive of the gale pushing him toward the south. The net result of the conflicting forces placed the *Portland* off Cape Cod early the next day.

At five forty-five that Sunday morning, Keeper A. C. Fisher of the Race Point Coast Guard Station heard four blasts from

---

* My mother, Alice Rowe Snow, could always "box the compass," or recite the thirty-two points. The cardinal points are North, East, South, and West, with each divided into eight identifications. Mother would begin, "North, North by East, North North East, Northeast by North, Northeast, Northeast by East, East Northeast, East by North," and then "East . . ." until she had included all thirty-two points.

a steamer's whistle. He went out, glanced at the clock, and rang the gong for the surfboat in case rescue work was ahead. Although he telephoned Peaked Hill Station to be on the lookout and sent a man down to the beach, neither ship nor wreckage could be seen at that time. "Conditions were the worst I have known," Keeper Fisher said later.

While Fisher and his men saw no sign of the *Portland* early that morning, when the eye of the hurricane passed across Cape Cod between nine and ten-thirty, causing a brief clearing in the sky, several other persons observed the *Portland* wallowing in the huge offshore seas some five to eight miles from Cape Cod. The clear weather lasted until ten-thirty, and then the storm returned with all its awesome fury. By two o'clock it was worse than ever.

At the end of the afternoon, the bitter wind continued to fill the air with snow and sand, making it nearly unbearable for Surfman John Johnson of the Peaked Hill Bars Station as he plodded along the beach. He knew that another lifesaver was pushing toward him from the Race Point Station several miles away and that ahead was the Half Way House which marked the division of their patrol. Arriving at the Half Way House, Johnson met his fellow watchman, Surfman Bickers, exchanged a story or two, spoke of the gale, and started back along the wind-swept beach.

The darkness increased. At seven-twenty Johnson thought he saw something thrown up by the incoming tide. Keeping his eye on the object, he fought his way down to the shore, picked up his find, and hastily retreated to the bank above the surf. In the dim light of his lantern he examined the object. It was a life belt, and on it he read the words *Steamer Portland of Portland*. He had no reason to suppose anything more than that the boat had lost a life preserver.

Here is his statement:

"I was bound west toward the station, when I found the

first thing that landed from the steamer. It was a life belt and it was one-half mile east of the station. At seven-forty-five o'clock that evening I found the next wreckage, a creamery can, forty-quart, I guess. It was right below our station, and nine or ten more of them, all empty and stoppered tightly came on there closely together.

"Jim Kelly succeeded me on the eastern beat, leaving the station at eight-twenty P.M. and at nine-thirty he found doors and other light woodwork from the *Portland* on the shore. When I found the life belt the wind was north northeast."

Actually, the *Portland* was at that time in the last stages of foundering. Thomas Harrison Eames, writing in the *New England Quarterly,** tells us that:

"It seems probable that the intense smashing she received through the night had weakened her, and finally the pounding of the seas under her guards opened her up and allowed tons of water to rush into the hull, flooding engine and boiler rooms, drowning the men at work there, and depriving the ship of her power. The passengers above must have experienced a sense of horrified dismay as the vibration of the engines stopped and the ship swung around broadside to the oncoming seas, lurching sickeningly and settling deeper each moment. The water crashing into the helpless vessel would smash any lifeboats which may have remained, tear off doors, and burst through windows and ports, ripping away the sheathing of the superstructure and washing helpless occupants of staterooms to death in a churning sea.

"As she took her final plunge, the superstructure was probably torn away at the main deck and was smashed to kindling wood. Those inside were thrown into the icy water as the wooden deckhouse disintegrated, some being killed outright by falling beams and other debris, others being caught in the

* Vol. XIII, No. 2, p. 194 (1940).

wreckage and carried under the surface to drown, while many who had equipped themselves with lifebelts or who succeeded in grasping floating wreckage were benumbed by the frigid water and hammered so unmercifully by the gigantic waves that they soon died."

It was not until eleven o'clock, around high tide, that the wreckage began to come ashore in large quantities. Edwin B. Tyler of the Race Point crew found doors, electric light bulbs, washstand tops, and other wreckage, and when the midnight watch returned, the beach was buried with debris from the *Portland*. Mattresses, chairs, upholstery, windows, doors, and paneling all came ashore just before midnight.

The next morning the Cape Cod shore was littered with wreckage piled eight and ten feet high. In with the *Portland*'s remains were fragments from the ninety-six-foot granite schooner *Addie E. Snow*, which had also gone down with all hands. A short distance away, the upper part of the cabin from the steamer *Pentagoet* was found embedded in the sand. Thirty-six bodies were eventually recovered and identified from the *Portland*, but not one body was ever found from either the *Snow* or the *Pentagoet*. The wreck of the *Snow* was discovered many years later a short distance from the *Portland* on the bottom of the sea.

Several watches, recovered from the bodies of the victims, had stopped at about nine-fifteen, and since the *Portland* was definitely seen afloat later than that on Sunday morning, we can safely assume that she made her final plunge at around quarter past nine that Sunday night, November 27, 1898.

Because the wreckage of the *Addie E. Snow* and the *Portland* came up on the beach together, it is entirely possible that a collision may have occurred between the two vessels. An engine room gong and clapper later floated to the surface on a bulkhead and was brought into Boston.* In order for

* I now own the gong, having received it eight years ago.

this to be freed from the engine room in the bowels of the ship, the *Portland* must have split open before she sank.

Many questions were solved on July 1, 1944, when diver Al George went to the bottom and visited the wreck of the steamer *Portland* at a point seven miles out to sea from the Race Point Coast Guard Station and about five miles across from Highland Light. As a result of his diving investigation we can say that the *Portland* probably collided with the *Addie E. Snow,* which lies on the bottom less than a quarter mile away from the *Portland.*

Writing in *Yankee* magazine for November 1956, I stated that not until October 1956 was the list of victims who drowned on the *Portland* complete at 190. Imagine my surprise three years later to receive a letter from Olive Prescott Digges of Newport News, Virginia, telling me that her father, George L. Prescott, was lost on the steamer *Portland.* His name, however, was not on the list of victims.

Thus the number who went down on the *Portland* becomes 191, and those of my readers who have *The Vengeful Sea* should add the name of Mr. Prescott to the list of victims on page 288.*

Several items which have come into my possession since my last book mentioning details of the vessel's loss include a life belt, a large milk container, and two metal baggage checks from the vessel.

The life belt was obtained from Osborn McArthur of Hyannis, who in turn received it from one of the family of Surfman John Johnson who found it on the beach the night of the *Portland* disaster.

The milk container was obtained several years ago for me by Mr. Russell Lawry of Lynnfield, and since then I have received the two *Portland* metal baggage checks.

An anchor, chain, and plates brought up from the steamer

* Also, the name of John McKay should be listed Mackey.

Portland by a dragger are now on exhibition on the lawn of a hotel at Martha's Vineyard. I am told that the owner is Ernesto A. Balla of New Bedford.

One of the most persistent objectors to my statement that the *Portland* went down in 1898 is a lady who quotes her family Bible as saying that the date should be 1896. Nothing I can say regarding the daily accounts of newspapers of the period will change her viewpoint. Then there are many who claim no other craft ever sighted the *Portland* after she sailed, which, of course, is ridiculous.

Another account of intense interest to those who follow the *Portland* saga is owned by Mrs. Faith Peterkin of Bryn Mawr, Pennsylvania. It is a journal which describes in vivid language the *Portland* disaster in which her father lost his brother George and a friend, E. Dudley Freeman.

Excerpts from the journal of Dr. William B. Kenniston, her father, follow. They were written at Yarmouth, Maine.

"Dec. 31, 1898

"Since my last writing in this book I have lived long and much. My life which at that time was running on smoothly and pleasantly and in a way that seemed likely to continue as long as I remained in Yarmouth has been changed completely. On Sunday, November 27th I lost my brother George and my most intimate friend, Hon. E. Dudley Freeman, and I have not yet become adjusted to the new condition.

"Father, Mother and Alice left Maine early in November for a two months trip through the west and Mabel had invited George and me to spend Thanksgiving with her and Emerson at Hyde Park [Massachusetts]. My business was such that I could not go, but George took the boat from Bath to Boston on Tuesday night November 22nd with several other Bowdoin boys, and spent the rest of the week with Mabel— and a very happy week, too. He was anxious to see me before getting back to college and when I found I could not go to Hyde Park we arranged for him to come by boat to Portland Saturday night and spend Sunday with me. Accordingly on Saturday night—after a very happy afternoon with Mabel and Bess at the theatre, he went to the boat. It was the Steamer *Portland* the largest and best boat of the line * which was then known as the Portland Steam Packet Company. She left the wharf on her regular sailing hour—7 o'clock and was seen off Thacher's Island about 9:30—and seen no more—except in such fragments as the miserly sea has thrown up.

"Burned into my mind in a way I shall never forget is every detail of those days. Saturday was a typical 'day before a snow-storm.' I remember it distinctly and every look of the sky for I had plenty of leisure during the intervals of attending a confinement case to observe the weather. . . . That evening it was just beginning to snow as I drove into the stable and I thought of George and the Boston boat but did not worry for I remembered the well-known caution of the Company and decided the boat did not sail.

"Sunday morning there was a blizzard raging when I awoke and again I thought of George and expressed my slight anxiety to Mr. Bucknam who assured me that there was not a possible chance that the boat had sailed. Snow was piled up outside and had not ceased falling. The wind was blowing a hurricane and the cold was intense. As I had been away so much of the day before there were several patients whom I had to see. After breakfast I put the saddle on 'Gyp' and with my case slung across my shoulders made a few necessary calls. As I went by the Freeman's Mrs. Freeman came to the door and waved her hand to me and the girls, Mary and Constance, watched me from the window. I looked for Mr. Freeman for I had expected him the night before.

"After dinner I waded through the snow to the Freeman's

* See John C. Poland's remarks below.

planning to spend the afternoon smoking and chatting with Mr. Freeman. To my surprise I found he had not arrived but was to have come by the boat from Boston. Mrs. Freeman and I talked the matter over and were perhaps a bit anxious but decided not to worry for the boat doubtless did not leave. In the evening again I went over to the Freeman's and took supper. . . .

"Monday morning I waited in Mr. Bucknam's store for the papers before making my round and to my delight I saw in the Press that the Str. *Portland* had not sailed. This relieved me of all worriment and I took the paper over to Mrs. Freeman at once. Again I made my rounds on horseback, in the forenoon and not till late in the afternoon were the roads broken out enough to make the sleighs possible.

"About half past seven in the evening Mrs. Freeman came to my office and said she was nervous and worried. She had not heard from Mr. Freeman. She had thought the reason for this might be that the wires were down, but she had just been to the Station and the wires from Boston were working all right. Now Mr. Freeman was a man who was in the habit of telegraphing whenever he was delayed or was called away unexpectedly and we could not understand why he should not send word now. Naturally we both thought of the Str. *Portland* once more and wondered if the report in the paper was false. . . . Finally to settle matters I said I would go down to the Store and telephone to Portland to the office of the Company and inquire just what was known of the boat, and started at once.

"Awaiting me at the Store was a telegram, as follows—

" 'Str. Portland left Boston Saturday night—George aboard —very anxious.' signed Emerson Rice. The Steamer then had indeed sailed. I telephoned at once to the office of the Company at Portland and asked for news. They knew nothing but gave the hope that she was either blown to Sea or was in

Provincetown Harbor, that port not having been heard from. I dreaded to go back to Mrs. Freeman with my unfavorable news and waited in my office and paced up and down Portland St. till I was able to control myself. . . . I told Mrs. Freeman of my telegram and what I had learned from the Company. I tried to comfort and cheer the poor woman but I fear it was a poor encouragement I was able to give. About 11:30 I left her promising to return early in the morning or when I heard any news. From Mrs. Freeman's I went to the Station and telegraphed to the Press in Portland for news. None had been received. Again at five o'clock I telegraphed with the same result. Then I went to Mrs. Freeman's and got from her the names of those people whom she would want notified if I did not get any favorable news and on the first train I went into Portland.

"Nothing had been heard at the office of the Steamboat Company and it was an anxious sad looking crowd that waited there breathless all the forenoon. . . . After lunch of a cup of coffee I went again to the offices of the Company where I found news had just been received. The *Portland* was wrecked off Truro Cape Cod and all on board were lost. . . ."

[After borrowing money, as his father was away and he did not know how much he might need, Dr. Kenniston went to Boston with his friend Mr. Bucknam, spending Tuesday night in Hyde Park with his sister, Mrs. Emerson Rice.]

"On Wednesday morning Mr. Bucknam was told all bodies found were to be brought to Boston for identification. The morning papers stated that seventeen bodies had been recovered, the first one found being that of Mr. Freeman. I returned to Boston about noon and waited all day at the offices for the tug that was to bring the bodies. Finally tired out I took a room at the Parker House, leaving word with the Steamboat Company to notify me of anything new. About eight o'clock I was called up by telephone and was told that the tug would bring no bodies and that I must go to the Cape to identify those found.

"After breakfast Thursday morning I took the eight o'clock train for the Cape. When twenty miles from Boston evidence of the fierceness of the storm was visible on every hand. Wires were down with many of the poles blown flat. Trees had been blown across the track frequently. This was the first train of the week for the Cape. Chimneys on every hand were seen lying on the ground and occasionally a house or more frequently a barn could be seen in ruins from the gale. After getting upon the Cape the violence of the storm was even more apparent. There the ground was bare and a more desolate barren region I hope I never see again. The trees of the Cape are a scrub oak and a stunted pine, and these with the almost complete lack of tillage make a most dreary landscape.

"At one place the track, although some miles from the sea, had been washed out and the passengers of the train were transported for three miles to Sandwich in carriages. When leaving the train to take the carriage I met Frank Mills Blair who had been to Provincetown and seen all but one of the bodies. He told me that John H. Dollof of Chatham, formerly of Boothbay had seen that, and it was not ours. I was relieved not to have to go to Provincetown.

"Our destination was Orleans where we arrived about 2 o'clock. After a hurried dinner Dr. Thompson and I went to the office of Medical Examiner Davis and then drove to the shop of Undertaker Steele. The shop had not been large enough and Undertaker Steele had made use of an adjoining shed for a temporary morgue. There were nine bodies lying on low improvised tables covered each with a sheet. We asked to see the body identified as Mr. Freeman. There was no doubt of the identification.

"One by one Mr. Steele lifted the sheet from the other eight and I scanned each one fearing yet dreading to find

George. None of us found those we sought, and we once more took our carriage and drove to Undertaker Mayo's where in a similar shed were eight more victims—but none that belonged to any of us.

"Never shall I forget the scenes of that awful day. We were not alone in our search for our dead, nor were we the only ones unsuccessful. Of the two hundred persons on that ill-fated Steamer to this day only thirty-three have been found. By far the greater number of those who went to the Cape in quest of lost friends or relatives returned emptyhanded, and heartbroken.

"I arranged to take the body of Mr. Freeman to Yarmouth, and asked Mr. Dollof to view every body found where there was the slightest chance of its being my brother. He did so, but with no result. There was a false report that George's body had been found, so I returned to Boston on Saturday, but returned to Yarmouth on Monday. . . ."

When Dr. Kenniston went back to Yarmouth he returned to the routine of his medical practice.

In my thirty-four years of lecturing I have told the story of the *Portland* hundreds of times, and always the account of the beautiful white and gold steamer's sailing and the tragedy of her loss have moved the audience deeply. After my lectures the people in the audience have come forward to see and touch a model of the *Portland,** the engine room gong, the wooden stateroom fittings, a forty-quart milk can, the old life preserver, or the flag belonging to the steamer.

Many a story I have been told of people who sailed on the vessel that fatal night or on more pleasant occasions.† Some

* Made and presented to me by John H. Dodge of Rhode Island. The model has been seen by tens of thousands of people.

† Some of my notes have been lost, and I still would appreciate receiving letters from those readers who have stories to tell about the *Portland*.

individuals planned to go aboard but missed the boat by having a last drink at a nearby bar. Others were delayed by the breakdown of a trolley car. At least one passenger, a Mr. Gott of Brooklyn, Maine, was said to have disembarked after observing the ship's cat making several trips down the gangway with a different kitten in her mouth each time until her litter was all ashore, as she deserted the ship.

Mrs. Anna Young of Boston was in her stateroom when she received a message from her mother that she was to leave the ship at once. Grabbing her child, Mrs. Young rushed to the gangplank just as they were about to lift it and went ashore. Her mother had a premonition that she should not sail, and she didn't.

As a member of the Boston Marine Society I often sat and listened as the old sea captains discussed the Portland storm. Without exception, each sailing master backed the decision of Captain Hollis H. Blanchard. He was told to sail by the officials of the Portland Steam Packet Company, and sail he did to his death. It is so easy for officers of a shipping company to claim after a disaster that they had given the captain his choice, but all members of the marine society were unanimous in saying that the captain, to keep his job, carried out his orders to sail.*

Each year observances both private and public have been held on the anniversary of the sinking of the Portland in memory of the passengers and crew who lost their lives. When the forty-seventh annual service took place in Boston in 1945, John C. Poland and his wife, now of Camden, Maine, were

---

* The six master mariners in the discussion were Captains Frank H. Peterson, Orville S. Pinkham, Eugene S. McKown, Odber R. Farrell, Charles T. Snow, and William J. Keating.

A later similar case was that of Captain Piero Calamai of the *Andrea Doria* who in 1956 was proceeding through the fog much faster than common sense would dictate when the fatal crash took place with the *Stockholm*. The *Doria* sank. The owners have always insisted on keeping schedules.

present. Mr. Poland is one of the dedicated men who love to reminisce on the now-forgotten days of steamboats, which at one time ran up and down the Maine coast. That night of 1945 I asked him to recall on paper his memories of the happier days of the steamer *Portland,* and later he sent me his thoughts.

"The SS *Portland* of the old 'Portland Steampacket Co.' was one of my favorite ships as a boy. I have pictures of it gleaned from this and that travel-gazetteer of those early years, back in the 1890's. And I well remember that awful day when news came that 'the Portland was lost'; it was as though some old friend had died.

"My folks came from Maine and we spent our vacation days down there. Sometimes we went by train, taking the cars at the old railroad station in Haymarket Square; but equally often we took the 'Portland boat' from India Wharf. We usually took the little old open-car electrics from Park Square (we had gone in on the 5:20 train from West Roxbury Station) and jogged our way to Atlantic Avenue. Sometimes when I was with my older brother we walked the distance across Boston and enroute passed down through Broad Street where (to this day, over seventy years later, in memory) I smelled the coffee being ground and bagged. As we approached the wharf we saw the big steamer backed-up toward the Avenue and wearing a large canvas sign hanging down from the top deck bearing the information 'This steamer sails tonight at 7 o'clock for Portland. Fare $1.'

"It was always a joy going 'down on the boat.' To my childish eyes the ship was enormous! And yet, so was our horse, Dan, a *big animal;* and when I learned that Dan was going on the boat, too, I was a bit fearful lest he be too much for even those vessels. The very gangplank leading into the fairy-palace was a promise of greater promise to come. And the insides with the grand staircases, the carpeted floors, the plush chairs and larger seats, the open forward saloon with its gallery above, and the staterooms with those interesting bunks, one smaller over a larger beneath, and the people coming and going: all these experiences for a boy of from four to twelve years of age were foretastes of a sort of heaven. For I can't remember when I actually *began* to sail on the *Portland*, but I was over twelve when she sailed out on her last voyage. I suspect I was carried aboard as a babe-in-arms at first.

"But I do remember this: I must have just passed my sixth birthday and was very proud and conscious of my increasing years. I was with my mother out in the saloon and there were other passengers and friends moving about, and a ship's officer (the Purser most likely) came around threading his way between folks and collecting the fares.

"And I remember this too: As we made our way about there in that big saloon we had to walk around mattresses being laid out on the floor. I can still 'see' folks standing by their allotted mattresses, perhaps lying on them, so great was the demand for space in those busy years.

"Once in our own stateroom mother always rang the bell for the stewardess to fetch us a pitcher of ice-water; for we brought our own supper. I can't remember ever having gone into the dining-saloon. And there seated on the one stool or on the edge of the berths we munched our sandwiches and had our cakes and drank the ice-water. But *that* was like a picnic. And what boy ever scorned a picnic? And mother, and Bertha, and Etta and Willard made it all a bit of home right there in our cabin. It was a lark! But the hour passed; and as we sat there eating suddenly someone said: 'Look! The wharf is sliding backward!' And sure enough it was slowly moving along and with definitely gathering speed. And then the great and deep-throated whistle boomed somewhere overhead to announce to all in front of the wharf's slip that the steamer was going forth, and to watch out. And we could now hear the slap-slap-slap of the big paddles on the wheel.

"No boy is ever satisfied to remain cooped-up, no matter how glamorous was the stateroom at first, nor, for that matter the grand saloon either. The open deck was the goal. And it was not only the bow-deck; it was all over the boat from top to bottom. And probably the section most interesting was where the walking-beam was working so gallantly and forcefully: the one end-rod going constantly up-and-down, up-and-down, and the other rod likewise up-and-down but with a swinging motion that was describing a circle somewhere out of sight down below, as it pulled and pushed on the paddle-wheel crank. And all the while the giant triangles of iron rocked up and down across a balancing center cross-beam. Oh, you could watch that a long time and never tire. But I remember seeing other things there too (and for a long time, years, I had thought I must have been mistaken in that memory) for *there,* from the two masts, were booms with sails tied down on each. At the time I probably thought nothing of it; in after years I had begun to wonder: 'Now, what would sails be doing on a steamship? Could I have seen aright?' Yes I did see aright. I was witnessing those final scenes when steamboat companies were considerate of the fears of their passengers lest something happen to the engine and the boat become 'lost' at sea; the Company had their steamers *wear sails,* just in case! Ah, that is a precious thought. I wasn't born too late.

"I remember watching the end of the wharf recede into the gathering dusk till it became a mere pin-point. We were on our way down the harbor. The smell of the water-washed shores of the passing islands is with me yet. The beacons that guided us through the dredged channels shone brightly ahead the one just a bit above and behind the other. The noises and calls from passing craft and the harbor lights (that queer one on steel legs, 'Bug Light' more exactly called the Narrows Light, and then that tall white tower, [Boston Light] stately and beautiful, at the corner where the steamer turned up, toward Maine) all were a part of the ever new fairyland so dear to childhood.

" 'Oh well, *I just loosen my corsets,*' told my mother to friends; 'I never undress aboard the steamer.' I don't remember just what a boy did. And so the night passed. But the wonted creakings and jarring noises were music to a boy's ears and probably he went to sleep listening to the symphony of the ship. But early in the morning as the *Portland* glided in toward Franklin Wharf there over toward the right I remember seeing a bluish, lofty, ghostly structure the sides of which came up and ended in a semi-circular roofing. It was the old Grand Trunk depot.

"Now in later years as we sailed on in the night and approached Boon Island light we always looked for 'the other boat' on *its* way to Boston. And from the *Dingley* there soon sputtered forth from somewhere just over the Pilot House a streak of light that reached forth over the waters and swung up and down and then toward the passing sister-ship, *The Bay State:* and the other boat did the same. Then we both flashed an up-and-down good-night. But from the *Portland* I am not sure about this; whether there ever was in those earlier 1890's anything more than an eagle perched decoratively over the Pilot House; the day of the searchlight may not have arrived. Besides, the other boat then was the *Tremont.* And I have sailed with her too. And I recollect that one peculiar bit of fascination on her was the plate glass panel-window in the grand saloon that permitted the passengers to watch the workings of the engine.

JOHN C. POLAND"

Of course, there is still much that we should like to know for certain about the final day of the paddle-wheeler *Portland,* but the chances for new vital information seventy years after the *Portland* sank are indeed remote. In any case, her last voyage will forever remain New England's greatest saga of the sea.

INDEX

INDEX